Building Basic Skills in Reading

Book 2

Contemporary Books, Inc.
Chicago

Library of Congress Cataloging in Publication Data
Main entry under title:

Building basic skills in reading.

    1. English languge—Grammar—1950-
    2. Basic education   I. Contemporary Books, inc.
PE1126.A4B8   428.6   81-804
ISBN 0-8092-5840-4 (pbk.)

Published by Contemporary Books, Inc.
180 North Michigan Avenue, Chicago, Illinois 60601
Manufactured in the United States of America
Library of Congress Catalog Card Number: 81-804
International Standard Book Number: 0-8092-5840-4

Published simultaneously in Canada by Beaverbooks, Ltd.
195 Allstate Parkway, Valleywood Business Park
Markham, Ontario L3R 4T8 Canada

ACKNOWLEDGMENTS

The thoughtful efforts of a great many people went into the preparation of Contemporary Books' *Building Basic Skills* series. We gratefully acknowledge their contributions and continued involvement in Adult Education.

Adult Education Division

Lillian J. Fleming, Editorial Director
Barbara Drazin, Editor
Wendy Harris, Marketing Services Coordinator

Production Department

Deborah Eisel, Production Editor

Reading and Readability Editors

Jane L. Evanson   Deborah Nathan
Helen B. Ward   Jane Friedland
Norma Libman   Donna Wynbrandt

Authors and Contributors

Writing: Rob Sax

Social Studies: Robert Schambier
                Carol Hagel
                Phil Smolik
                Jack Lesar
                Nora Ishibashi
                Helen T. Bryant
                Jo Ann Kawell
                Deborah Brewster
                Mary E. Bromage
                Sheldon B. Silver
                Patricia Miripol

Science: Ronald LeMay
         Cynthia Talbert
         Jeffrey Miripol
         John Gloor
         William Collien
         Charles Nissim-Sabat

Reading: Timothy A. Foote
         Raymond Traynor
         Pamela D. Drell (Editor)

Mathematics: Jerry Howett

Project Assistance
    Sara Plath

Graphic Art: Louise Hodges
Cover Design: Jeff Barnes

CONTENTS

1 CRITICAL READING

2 PRACTICAL READING: FOLLOWING WRITTEN DIRECTIONS

TO THE LEARNER

Building Basic Skills in Reading, Books 1 and 2 will give you, the learner, all you need to master the basics of reading well. Together, the books give a complete program that is easy to use on your own or with a teacher in class.

The following chart shows the reading skills covered in each book.

BUILDING BASIC SKILLS IN READING	
Book 1	Book 2

Understanding Paragraphs
    Main Idea: Stated and
        Unstated
    Supporting Details
 	
How Details Are Arranged
    Sequence
    Relationships
        Cause and Effect
        Comparison and
        Contrast
        Rank of Importance
 	
Learning New Words When
  Reading
    Context
    Synonyms and Antonyms
    Examples and Descriptions
    Root Words, Prefixes and
        Suffixes
    Compound Words
 	
Making Inferences
	Critical Reading
	    Facts and Opinions
	    Bias
	    Propaganda
	    Style and Tone
	
	Practical Reading—Following
	    Written Directions
	
	Practical Reading—Charts and
	    Illustrations
	    Diagrams
	    Charts
	    Listings and Schedules
	    Graphs

HOW TO USE THIS BOOK

Each unit of *Building Basic Skills in Reading* has plenty of exercises to give you practice in the reading skills covered. The exercises have questions for you to answer. All answers are in the answer section at the end of each unit. You will be able to check your work quickly and easily using this section.

Each unit also ends with a few Review Exercises. These Review Exercises will cover all the new ideas presented in the unit.

Before you begin working, you should start with the **Pre-Test.** This test will show you how much you already know about the skills that are covered in the book. Don't expect to get every answer right on the Pre-Test. If you do, there's no reason for you to read this book! After you take the Pre-Test fill in the Skill Mastery Chart on page 11.

At the very end of the book there is a **Post-Test** which has questions from all of the units. If you understand the units, you should do very well on this test. After you take the Post-Test, fill in the Skill Mastery Chart on page 151. By that time you will be able to look at how you did on both the Pre- and Post-Tests. This will show how much stronger your reading skills have become.

WHY ARE READING SKILLS IMPORTANT?

Reading is one of the most important skills a person can have in life. Being a good reader makes getting and keeping a good job easier. Having good reading skills makes learning about new things much easier. You can get through life not being able to read, but many things are easier if you can read well.

There are many reading skills. Part of reading is knowing what words look like written down and being able to figure out new words. But reading also means sorting out what you have read and understanding what the writer's purpose is. A lot of reading is thinking about the words on the page. That is hard unless you can easily understand them.

The work in *Building Basic Skills in Reading* is meant to be fun and interesting as well as helpful. The examples, exercises, reviews and tests will build your basic reading skills and pave the way for you to go on to higher levels of reading and learning. We hope you enjoy your work.

The Editors of Contemporary Books

PRE-TEST

Directions: The purpose of the Pre-Test is to show you the kind of work you will be doing in *Building Basic Skills in Reading, Book 2*. It will also give you an idea of how much you already know about the skills that will be covered.

   The Pre-Test has a total of 33 questions. There is no time limit for the test. You can take a break while you're working on it. When you're done, check your answers starting on page 9. Then fill in the Mastery Skill Chart on page 11.

Read the following directions. Then answer the questions.

Installing Your Kleen-flow Oil Filter

Congratulations! You have just bought the world's best oil filter—the Kleen-flow. You will never need to buy another filter. The Kleen-flow will last for the life of your car. It will cost you only pennies with each oil change.

To Remove Your Old Filter: Unscrew the filter, turning it to the left. Clean the spot where the filter screws onto the engine. Throw away the old filter.

To Install Your Kleen-flow: After taking your new Kleen-flow out of the box, turn the filter upside down.

Insert a roll of toilet paper into the Kleen-flow filter. Any kind will do. Just make sure the roll has 1,000 sheets and is loosely wound. If the end of the toilet paper is loose, use some tape to hold it down.

Next, spread a film of clean oil on the cork ring (which is called the gasket) in the bottom of your Kleen-flow. Screw the Kleen-flow onto the engine by hand only. Use no tools. Make sure it is tight.

Now unscrew the Kleen-flow again, until it is loose. Then tighten it again. After it is tight, give it one-half turn more. Do not go beyond one-half turn.

Run your engine for five minutes. Check around the bottom of your Kleen-flow for any leaks.

Do this every time you put in a new roll of toilet paper. You should change rolls every time you change oil.

Note: Most cars will take an extra quart of oil whenever a new filter is put in.

The following are steps you must take in changing Kleen-flow filters. They are in a scrambled order. Put them in the right order. Write the number 1 after the number of the step that comes first. Write 2 after the second step, and so on. Read all ten steps first. You may look back at the directions.

1. _____   Put in the roll of toilet paper.

2. _____   Clean the spot where the filter goes onto the engine.

3. _____   Take the new filter from the box and turn it upside down.

4. _____   Take off the old filter by turning it to the left.

5. _____   Tape the end of the toilet paper roll.

6. _____ Spread a film of clean oil on the cork ring of the new Kleen-flow filter.

7. _____ Run your engine for five minutes to check for leaks.

8. _____ Screw the filter on tightly by hand the first time.

9. _____ Loosen the filter and screw it on a second time.

10. _____ Throw away the old filter.

Use this chart to answer questions 11–15.
Put a check in front of the correct answer.

Temperatures on December 12		
City	High	Low
Cleveland	37°	31°
Columbia, S.C.	60°	27°
Columbus, Ohio	41°	34°
Dallas	81°	50°
Dayton	41°	33°
Decatur	39°	30°
Denver	49°	33°
Des Moines	34°	27°
Detroit	37°	28°
Dubuque	30°	23°
Duluth	19°	10°
Eau Claire	24°	19°
El Paso	79°	36°
Evansville	52°	36°
Fairbanks	−31°	−40°
Fargo	17°	−2°
Flint	31°	26°
Flagstaff	56°	31°
Great Falls	14°	3°
Grand Rapids	33°	26°
Green Bay	24°	20°

11.   What was the high temperature in Columbus, Ohio on December 12?

_____(1)   81°

_____(2)   50°

_____(3)   41°

_____(4)   60°

_____(5)   39°

12.   What was the low temperature in Flagstaff on this day?

_____(1)   26°

_____(2)   −2°

_____(3)   3°

_____(4)   56°

_____(5)   31°

13.   Which city had the highest temperature on this day?

_____(1)   El Paso

_____(2)   Dallas

_____(3)   Dayton

_____(4)   Great Falls

_____(5)   Green Bay

14.   Which city had the lowest temperature?

_____(1)   Des Moines

_____(2)   Flint

_____(3)   Fairbanks

_____(4)   Duluth

_____(5)   Eau Claire

15.   How many cities had a temperature below 0° sometime during the day?

_____(1)   one city

_____(2)   two cities

_____(3)   three cities

_____(4)   four cities

_____(5)   five cities

Read the following short story very carefully. After the story are 15 statements. Decide if each is true or false. If the statement is true, write true in the blank in front of the statement. If it is false, write false. If you can't tell from the story whether the statement is true or not, write not sure in the blank.

The night was cold and rainy. The movie let out at 11:30. Two children came out of the door and stood in front of the movie theater. The sign in front read, "Now Playing: Monster from the Deep."

The smaller child looked up at the bigger one. "Eddie, I'm scared."

The bigger one tried to push the smaller one away. "Don't be a chicken, Frank. The thing ain't real."

Frank tried to grab Eddie's hand. "I'm still scared. Do we have to walk home?"

"How else are we going to get there, stupid?"

"Couldn't we call and have someone come and get us?"

"They'd just get mad at us. Besides, it's only six blocks. And no one will get you, chicken."

Frank shivered. "I ain't no chicken, but I'm still scared."

"Come on," Eddie said. He took Frank by the hand. They set off into the dark night.

They ran the first two blocks, but slowed to a walk at the third block.

In the fourth block they heard a scream coming from an apartment window. The smaller child held tightly to the bigger one. They broke into a run again. The smaller child fell behind the bigger one.

The smaller one stumbled. "Eddie! Eddie! Wait for me."

Eddie kept running. At the start of the fifth block he stopped and looked back. Frank caught up to Eddie.

A woman was walking toward them from the other way. The children ran toward her. They were safe and no monsters had gotten them.

_____16.   It was a cold and rainy night.

_____17.   The two children had just seen the movie.

_____18.   A picture called, "Monster from the Deep," was showing at the theater.

_____19.   Eddie was the bigger and older brother of the two.

_____20.   Frank is afraid of the monster movie.

_____21.   The boys plan to call a cab to take them home.

_____22.   Eddie suggests that they call home to get a ride.

_____23.   The boys have six blocks to go to get home.

_____24.   The two of them ran the first four blocks.

_____25. The sound of someone screaming for help scared the two boys.

_____26. Eddie ran ahead of Frank after they heard the noise.

_____27. Frank fell and cried for Eddie to stop and wait.

_____28. Frank caught up with Eddie again in the fifth block.

_____29. The boys' mother was walking toward them.

_____

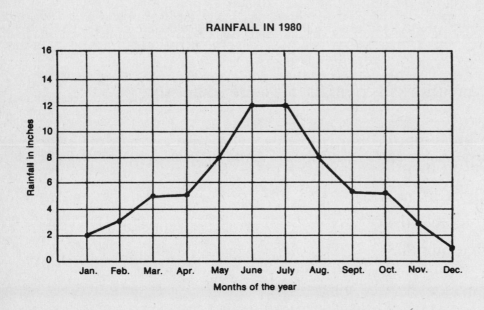

RAINFALL IN 1980

Put a check in front of the correct answer.

30. Which months had the biggest rainfall?
   _____(1) August and September
   _____(2) June and July
   _____(3) May and June
   _____(4) July and August
   _____(5) April and June

31.   Which month had the least rainfall?
_____(1)   January
_____(2)   October
_____(3)   December
_____(4)   February
_____(5)   March

32.   How many inches of rain fell in August?
_____(1)   nine inches
_____(2)   seven inches
_____(3)   ten inches
_____(4)   six inches
_____(5)   eight inches

33.   How many months had rainfall of more than six inches?
_____(1)   eight months
_____(2)   seven months
_____(3)   three months
_____(4)   four months
_____(5)   five months

ANSWERS & EXPLANATIONS — PRE-TEST

1. Take off the old filter by turning it to the left.
2. Clean the spot where the filter goes on to the engine.
3. Throw away old filter.
4. Take the new filter from the box and turn it upside down.
5. Put in the roll of toilet paper.
6. Tape the end of the toilet paper roll.
7. Spread a film of clean oil on the cork ring of the new filter.
8. Screw the filter on tightly by hand the first time.
9. Loosen the filter and screw it on a second time.
10. Run your engine for five minutes to check for leaks.

11. (3) 41°
12. (5) 31°
13. (2) Dallas
14. (3) Fairbanks
15. (2) two cities

16. True. The story says this.
17. Not sure. The children had just come out of the door. We don't definitely know they had seen the movie.
18. True. The story says this.
19. Not sure. Eddie is bigger. But nothing in the story says the two are brothers.

20. Not sure. Frank is afraid of some kind of monster. But we don't know that it's the monster from the film.
21. False. Frank wants to call someone at home, not a cab.
22. False. Frank suggests calling.
23. True. The story says this.
24. False. They ran two blocks.
25. Not sure. We don't know if the person they heard was screaming for help.

26. True. The story says this.
27. Not sure. Frank stumbled, but the story doesn't say that he fell down. It only says he fell behind.
28. True. The story says this.
29. Not sure. We don't know if the woman was their mother. The story really doesn't say.

30. (2) June and July
31. (3) December
32. (5) eight inches
33. (4) four months

PRE-TEST SKILL MASTERY CHART

Directions: Fill in the Skill Mastery Chart after you have checked your answers on the Pre-Test. Each skill on the test is listed with the test questions using that skill. Circle each question you answered correctly. Then count your total number of circled answers and write this in the box under Number Correct. Next, find the Skill Mastery Level that fits your number correct. Place a check (✔) in the box at the correct level. Do this for each skill listed. Then find your total number of correct answers and total number of checks at each Skill Mastery Level. The Skill Mastery Chart will tell you which skills you should work with most in this book.

SKILL	TOTAL SCORE	NUMBER CORRECT	SKILL MASTERY LEVELS			STUDY PAGES
			SKILL MASTERY	PRACTICE & REVIEW NEEDED	FULL LEARNING NEEDED	
			(Check one box in each row)			
1 Critical Reading 16, 17, 18, 19, 20, 21, 22 23, 24, 25, 26, 27, 28, 29	14		14-9	8-5	4-0	13-52
2 Following Directions 1, 2, 3, 4, 5 6, 7, 8, 9, 10	10		10-8	7-4	3-0	53-94
3 Charts/Graphs/Diagrams 11, 12, 13, 14, 15 30, 31, 32, 33	9		9-7	6-4	3-0	95-137
TOTAL	33					

1 CRITICAL READING

Reading is more than just knowing what the writer is telling you. This unit is about **critical reading.** To read critically means that you don't necessarily believe everything the writer tells you. It means that you think about what the writer says. <u>You</u> decide whether what he or she is saying is right or wrong. <u>You</u> decide if the writer is making sense or not. Unless you can think critically about what you read, you are hardly any better off than if you don't know what the words mean. Unless you are a critical reader, you won't be thinking for yourself. You will be letting the writer do all the thinking for you.

One of the most important parts of critical reading is thinking about what the writer's purpose is. Writers don't write just to pass the time. They write to entertain people or to frighten them or to make them believe certain things. Writers are very often trying to persuade their readers. They are trying to bring them around to their own way of looking at the world.

In this unit we will talk about different purposes that writers might have and the different ways that writers try to persuade their readers. The exercises in this unit will help you to think for yourself when you read.

SORTING OUT FACTS AND OPINIONS

Like you and me, writers have their own opinions. To choose between what you believe and what a writer would like you to believe, you must be able to tell the difference between fact and opinion.

Ads, political posters, newspaper editorials and magazine articles try to get you to think a certain way about things. As you read you should always be asking yourself "What would this writer like me to think? What do I, myself, think?" An important part of figuring out the answers to these questions is knowing what is fact and what is opinion.

What's the difference between fact and opinion? We all have a lot of both of them in our heads. Let's make a simple contrast:

(1)   A **fact** can be proved.

(2)   An **opinion** cannot be proved.

Imagine hearing the following conversation. As you read keep asking yourself: "What's fact? What's opinion?" Assume that each person is telling only the truth.

Secretary A: (1) The man I work for is the most demanding boss in the world. (fact or opinion?)

Secretary B: (2) I used to work for him. (fact or opinion?)

Secretary A: (3) You know what I'm talking about, then. (fact or opinion?) (4) This morning he gave me ten two-page letters to type before lunch. (fact or opinion?) (5) No one in the world can type that much in one morning. (fact or opinion?)

Secretary B: (6) When I worked for him, I never typed more than three letters a day. (fact or opinion?)

There are six sentences in the conversation you just read. Each one had a number in front of it. Three of them are facts. Three are opinions. In the blanks below write the numbers of the sentences that are facts (they can be proved) and the numbers of the sentences that are opinions.

Facts: ___ ___ ___

Opinions: ___ ___ ___

You should have written this:
Facts: _2_ _4_ _6_
Opinions: _1_ _3_ _5_

Let's see why the sentences should be divided in that way.

Remember: facts <u>can</u> be proved; opinions <u>cannot</u> be proved.

Sentence (1) is an opinion because there is no way to prove that the man is the most demanding boss in the world. Secretary A's opinion comes only from her own experience. She cannot have worked for every boss in the world.

Sentence (2) is a fact. If Secretary B worked for that man, it can be proved by checking records or by asking the boss.

Sentence (3) is an opinion. How can Secretary A know that Secretary B knows what she is talking about? She didn't ask her. (In fact, in Sentence (6) Secretary B shows she disagrees with Secretary A.)

Sentence (4) is a fact. By checking records it can be shown that ten letters <u>were</u> given to her.

Sentence (5) is an opinion. It would be impossible to prove that no one in the world could type ten letters in a morning. If even one person in the world <u>could</u>, it is not a fact.

Sentence (6) is a fact. It can be proved by checking work records or asking the boss.

Exercise 1

Read each of the following sentences. In the blanks by each, write "Fact" or "Opinion" to show what kind of statement it is.

_____(1)   Today is the coldest March 3rd ever recorded in Atlanta.

_____(2)   Chicken livers taste better than beef livers.

_____(3)   I've noticed that everyone is afraid of the amount of crime in this city.

_____(4)   A cup of sand weighs more than a cup of water.

_____(5)   My pay has doubled in the last six years.

Answers start on page 47.

People often use facts to come up with opinions. Or, they may have opinions and find facts to support them. Read the following three people's ideas about the best thing to do on a Sunday afternoon in summer.

Millie: The best way to spend a Sunday afternoon in summer is to go to the beach. You can soak up the sun. This is good for your health. It can be very relaxing to lie on a blanket and sweat. And swimming is such a good way to use your muscles.

Harry: Sunday afternoon in summer is best spent watching television. It can be exciting to watch sports or old movies. And it can be relaxing just to lie back and be entertained by whatever is on. It can be a lot cooler than being out in the sun.

Bea: I think the best way to spend an afternoon in summer is in church. There I can be with people who share my beliefs. I get strength and help from them as I look forward to a new week. I really enjoy the fellowship at my church.

In each example above, the person's opinion is stated in the first sentence. The opinions are then followed by facts and reasons.

The important thing to notice is that each person chooses the facts needed to make his or her opinion sound right. Millie, who likes to sit on the beach, talked about the value of being in the sun sweating and the swimming. Harry, who likes to watch television, uses entertainment, relaxation and coolness to make his opinion sound good. Bea talks of how good she feels with people who share her beliefs and give her strength.

Of course, each one is right as far as each speaker is concerned. But, to make the opinion sound right, the person leaves out the things that will not help support the opinion.

For example, Millie leaves out the idea that staying home and watching television can be entertaining. Harry leaves out the healthful benefits of the sun and swimming. Bea leaves out relaxation (either in the sun or in front of a television set) as a nice way to spend a Sunday afternoon.

So, each person chooses facts that will support his or her opinion.

SEEING A WRITER'S BIAS

When you read something, you must be aware that the writer may do the same thing as our three "Sunday afternoon people" did. If you are able to see how a writer uses facts to come to an opinion, you have found that writer's bias. The **bias** is the person's "leaning." A person may lean toward one opinion or another.

Pick up any newspaper any day and read the editorials. These articles are always statements of opinion from the owners of the newspaper.

Exercise 2

An editorial follows. See if you can find the writer's bias as you read it. Use your common sense to figure out which statements are probably fact. Assume that the writer doesn't write anything but the truth. Read the editorial. Answer the questions that follow it.

(1) The world is going to the dogs. The basic root of our American way of life is coming out of the ground! (2) When uprooted any growing plant will die! (3) The root of life is the family. (4) This plant—our family—is our whole society. (5) Its roots are coming out of the ground because of the divorce rate. (6) It is now true that half of all marriages end in divorce. (7) For every two weddings there will be one divorce. (8) Further, the rate of divorce is climbing. (9) Only ten years ago, the divorce rate was one out of three. (10) Now it is one out of two. (11) How soon will it be before every marriage ends in divorce?

(12) Our way of life will come to an end because the children of these broken marriages will have no stable home life. (13) They will grow up with unstable personalities. (14) That will make for a very unstable world.

1. In the editorial, there are only five sentences which can be proved to be fact. Which are they? Write the numbers of those five sentences here: _____ _____

_____ _____ _____

2. Put a check mark (✔) in front of all sentences that
    show the bias of the writer.

    _____(1)   The divorce rate in America is growing.

    _____(2)   A stable way of life in America can only be
                based on stable families.

    _____(3)   Divorce causes our world to weaken.

    _____(4)   Children of divorced parents are as stable
                as children whose parents don't divorce.

    _____(5)   For every two weddings there will be one
                divorce.

3. Does the writer suggest that our world is going to fall
    apart?

    _____(1)   Yes, the writer sounds worried about the
                world.

    _____(2)   No, the writer really believes the world
                will be saved.

    _____(3)   It isn't clear what the writer thinks.

    _____(4)   The writer makes no suggestions.

    _____(5)   The writer only gives us the facts.

Answers start on page 47.

Another writer could take the same facts and show a
very different bias. Read this:

Our world is getting more and more healthy! Life is
getting better and better. Possibilities for individual growth
are everywhere. This can be shown by the growing divorce
rate. Now, one out of two marriages ends in divorce. This is
a very good sign.

No longer are people content to make a decision and
never question it again. A woman may have married ten
years ago. She may have expected to depend on her husband
for support for the rest of her life. Since then, she has come

to see that she can get out there and make it by herself. She feels better about herself making it on her own.

A man who was once afraid to try something new now is more free. He doesn't have to chain himself to one job because he needs a steady income to support a family. He can try new things.

As men and women grow, their ideas change. Many find that marriage is no longer the best thing for them if they are to try new things and grow as people. As each person grows, our world and our way of life get better and better.

Now, we don't need to pick this editorial apart. It is important to see just one thing. This writer uses the rising divorce rate as a sign that the world is getting better. The writer believes that it is getting better and more healthy because people can try new ways to live. As you remember from the earlier editorial, that writer used the same rising divorce rate to say that the world is falling apart.

One fact—the same fact—in two different minds is used to build two different opinions. That is a very clear example of writers' bias.

Exercise 3

Read the passage. Answer the questions that follow it. The questions will ask you to see the difference between fact and opinion, or to find the writer's bias.

The "oldest profession in the world" is still with us. The people who work in the oldest profession, if they are women, are called by a number of names: streetwalkers, ladies of the night, call girls. If they are men, they are called hustlers, gigolos, studs. No matter what word is used, those who sell their bodies to other people for sex are and will be with us.

As long as there are people to buy, there will be people to sell. But, it is rarely legal. Yet, it goes on all around us.

Men and women, but mostly women, are often hauled off to jail for prostitution. They are harassed by police officers. They are looked down on by many other people. Yet, all they are trying to do is make a living by using the skills they have. They are no different from any other worker. All sell their skills for money.

Prostitution should be made legal. If it were, governments would get more tax money. State medical departments could do a better job of checking for health problems. Of course, prostitutes would have to be licensed. But all of this would help to rid the profession of the dangers to both sellers and buyers.

1. Which one of the following ideas from the passage could be a fact?
   _____(1) Prostitution is the oldest profession in the world.
   _____(2) Prostitution is rarely legal.
   _____(3) As long as there are people to buy, there will be people to sell.
   _____(4) All they are trying to do is make a living.
   _____(5) They are no different from any other worker.

2. The writer's bias is that
   _____(1) prostitutes are just a bunch of street-walkers, ladies of the night, hustlers and studs.
   _____(2) prostitution should be made legal because it would be better for most people involved.

_____(3)   since prostitution is illegal, all men and women who work at it are terrible criminals.

_____(4)   prostitutes bring down everybody's morals.

_____(5)   making prostitution legal will bring down our society.

3.   Which of the following is <u>not</u> one of the writer's opinions:

_____(1)   Prostitutes are skilled workers like other working people.

_____(2)   Prostitution will always exist.

_____(3)   Only women can be prostitutes.

_____(4)   Legalizing prostitution would mean more profit for the government.

_____(5)   State medical departments could check for health problems more easily if prostitutes were licensed.

Answers start on page 48.

Exercise 4

Read this passage. Again, watch for the writer's bias. Look for the facts used to support the writer's opinions. Answer the questions that follow.

Television isn't something our children need. In fact, television is something that should be kept away from children. Children naturally like TV. They like bright lights and moving pictures. They can sit for hours, hypnotized, in front of a TV screen. But just because they like it, does that mean that it is good for children? No, it does not.

The American child watches TV for an average of three hours everyday. One-third of the children in America watch TV for an average of six hours everyday. Think of that—six hours each and every day! That's almost half of a child's waking hours. Those are hours when a child could be outside playing, strengthening his or her body.

Even more importantly, a child could be reading during those six hours. Instead of mindlessly soaking up hours of silly, worthless trash, a child could be learning about other places and people. A child could be seeing the world through the eyes of a great writer.

A child who watches TV for hours every single day isn't a child who thinks for himself. He or she believes every word that comes from that little gray screen. Until we rescue our children from "the tube," we won't have children who can decide things for themselves.

1. Which one of these statements is a fact?
   _____(1) Children naturally like television.
   _____(2) Reading, is better than mindlessly watching "the tube."
   _____(3) A child who watches television for hours is not a child who thinks.

   _____(4) TV is something that should be kept away from children.
   _____(5) One-third of the children in America watch TV for an average of six hours everyday.

2. Which one of these statements best tells how the writer feels about TV?
   _____(1) Some TV shows are very educational.
   _____(2) Parents should let their children watch no more than three hours of TV each day.

_____(3) Time watching TV could be better spent doing other things.

_____(4) Television has both good and bad points.

_____(5) TV can show children how different people live.

3. Which one of these activities would the writer prefer for a child?

_____(1) playing outside

_____(2) watching TV

_____(3) seeing a movie

_____(4) listening to the radio

_____(5) sitting still

Answers start on page 48.

UNDERSTANDING PROPAGANDA

Writing that tries to make you think a certain way is called **propaganda.** You may have heard this word used in political situations. Many Americans will use the words "communist propaganda." At the same time, many communists will use the words "capitalist propaganda."

One of the tricks of a person who writes propaganda is to use loaded words. A **loaded word** is a word full of emotion.

Let's see how loaded words work.

Suppose this is true:

There were 1,000 more births in Chicago this year than last year.

That is a simple fact. There are no loaded words in that sentence. But, one writer might state the same fact this way:

Chicago saw an <u>alarming</u> <u>explosion</u> in the birthrate this year!

The two loaded words in that sentence are underlined. Each word is loaded in a negative way. Each carries a bad or negative emotion.

Alarming puts us on edge. Think of fire alarm, burglar alarm, or "The people were alarmed (scared or upset)."

Explosions are violent. They usually cause some harm.

The writer uses these two loaded words to make us worry about the high birthrate in Chicago. If nothing else, we are supposed to believe that something is wrong.

Another writer might state the same fact in this way:

> The stork blessed Chicagoans with 1,000 more births this year than last.

Again, the loaded words are underlined. Each word is loaded in a positive way. Each carries a good or pleasant emotion.

Storks are associated with the gift of a child. Gifts are nice.

Blessed means "given something good." Think of blessed with good health, or blessed are the peacemakers.

The writer uses the loaded words to make us take pleasure in the growing birthrate.

Exercise 5

Read the following sentences. Decide whether the sentence has a good or bad effect on your emotions. Write "good" or "bad" in the blank in front of the sentence. Then, find the loaded words in the sentences and underline them.

_____ 1. The ragged and smelly tramp died of exposure in his cardboard shack.

_____ 2. The meeting blew up into a storm of angry words.

_____ 3. Our town's pride and joy, the talented Miss Davis, won the annual dance contest.

_____ 4. This part of town is dirty, dreary and full of rundown buildings.

_____ 5. The day was bright and sparkling.

_____ 6. The angry mob hissed and booed.

_____ 7. The girl was a vision of loveliness.

_____ 8. Carol looked trim, tidy and neat in her nurse's uniform.

_____ 9. The terrible force of the blast hurled him 30 feet through the air.

_____ 10. My brother is such a slob; he doesn't clean the kitchen even when it's totally filthy.

Answers start on page 48.

A sentence can have a double load of words that have both good <u>and</u> bad effects. A writer may want you to have negative thoughts about one thing and positive thoughts about another. He will write to try to affect you. A newspaper headline might say:

GREEDY LANDLORDS BEAT HELPLESS
TENANTS IN RENT BATTLE

By this headline, the writer wants you to see the landlords as the bad guys—greedy—and the tenants as the good guys—helpless.

Exercise 6

Read this ad and answer the questions that follow.

Ladies . . .

Do you want to know the secret of holding on to your husband? Do you want to know what will convince him beyond a doubt? Do you want him to know you love him as much as you did the day you married him?

Well, Listen!

The secret is Gold Anew. It will take off all the dingy grime from the most important gold you have, your wedding ring. If your wedding ring is not as beautiful as it was the day he put it on your finger, something is wrong! What does he think when he sees a dirty wedding ring, the one he gave you? Maybe he thinks you don't care about him anymore.

Just Do This.

Buy a jar of Gold Anew. The gentle and loving creams will renew your gold ring to its original brightness and warmth. Before your very eyes you will see the change. And when he sees it, you will see the change in his eyes, too. He will know you care.

GOLD ANEW

1. The purpose of this ad is to get a person to buy a gold polish. To do that, the advertisement is written to touch the reader's emotions. What emotion is being touched?

    _____(1)   pity for someone suffering

    _____(2)   love of someone admired

    _____(3)   fear of losing someone important

    _____(4)   longing for something new

    _____(5)   none of the above

2. In the second part of the ad, there are many loaded words or phrases. The words or phrases are loaded to make the reader feel nervous or ashamed. List at least three of those loaded words or phrases.

(a) _____

_____

(b) _____

_____

(c) _____

_____

3. Find the loaded words or phrases that are positive in the last part of the ad. List at least three of them.

(a) _____

_____

(b) _____

_____

(c) _____

_____

Answers start on page 49.

Exercise 7

Read this short passage. Then answer the questions that follow.

It was years ago that doctors found that smoking is dangerous to health. A warning appears on every cigarette package sold in the United States. People who keep smoking must be stupid. Or, they must have a very strong death wish. Everyone knows smoking makes the lungs look like the insides of garbage cans. The heart can end up working like a clock running down. The voice box can get so diseased that it has to be removed.

If a walker or a driver ignores a stop sign, he can be killed. When a smoker ignores the stop sign on a cigarette package, the result can be the same.

1. Which is the best way to state the writer's feeling about smoking?
    _____(1) Smoking isn't dangerous to health.
    _____(2) Smoking might be dangerous to health.
    _____(3) Smoking is dangerous to health.
    _____(4) Smoking can be pleasurable.
    _____(5) Smoking is up to the individual.

2. These are some of the loaded words and phrases in this passage:

        stupid
        death wish
        garbage cans
        clock running down
        diseased

What kind of load do those words have?

_____(1) positive

_____(2) negative

_____(3) no load

_____(4) mixed load

_____(5) pleasant load

3. The writer compares warnings on cigarette packages to

_____(1) the inside of garbage cans

_____(2) stop signs

_____(3) a clock running down

_____(4) a voice box

_____(5) railroad crossing

4. According to the writer, what can happen to smokers who ignore cigarette package warnings?

_____(1) They could miss valuable coupons.

_____(2) They may not see percentages of tar and nicotine.

_____(3) Nothing much would happen to most of them.

_____(4) They could seriously endanger their lives.

_____(5) none of the above.

Answers start on page 50.

UNDERSTANDING STYLE AND TONE

Style and tone are tools a writer uses to persuade his reader of something without saying it straight out. **Style** simply means a way of doing or saying something. Just as there are different styles of clothing, there are different styles of writing and speaking. A writer will choose a style that seems right for the kind of information he wants to give the reader. The **tone** of a piece is the emotion it carries. A writer might not come right out and say, "I was very hurt by what Sue did to me." But by the words and details he chooses, he will let the reader know what his emotion was. Writers use style and tone to make what they are saying beautiful or funny or sad or touching. Part of critical reading is being able to see <u>why</u> a writer is using a particular style and tone.

STYLE

We all act and speak differently with different people. That is to say, we use different styles with different people. You speak differently to the minister of your church than to your five-year-old son. You probably speak a little differently to your boss at work than to your sister or brother. Writers use style in much the same way. A writer will write one way if he is trying to get ten-year-old boys to buy a certain brand of toy truck. He will write in another style if he is asking the people of a city to elect him mayor. We will look at these different styles:

(1) Formal and Informal Styles
(2) Detailed and General Styles
(3) Technical and Lyrical Styles

Looking at Formal and Informal Styles

We use informal styles of speaking when we talk to people we know well, our family and our close friends. An informal style is relaxed and familiar. Slang is sometimes used as a part of an informal style. It is never used as part of a formal style. We use a more formal style when speaking to people we don't know well. You might use a more formal style if you are speaking to your boss at work or to the minister of your church. Young people are expected to be more formal when they speak to their teachers or to adults. Here are some examples of formal and informal styles. In each example, the same thing is said formally and informally.

1. **Formal**: Good morning, Mr. Jones. How are you today?

   Informal: What's happening, Jones?

2. **Formal**: We would be delighted if you and your wife and children could join us for dinner this Sunday.

   Informal: Why don't you and the gang drop by for dinner on Sunday?

Exercise 8

Below are two lists of sentences—formal and informal. For each formal sentence pick the informal sentence that means the same thing. Write the letter of the matching sentence in the blank.

Formal Sentences	**Informal Sentences**
1. ___Would it annoy you if I were to smoke here?	(a) Got a dime?
2. ___Can you tell me how I might get to Caesar's Palace?	(b) What time do you have?
3. ___Excuse me, can you tell me what time it is?	(c) Mind if I smoke?
4. ___You may all be seated. Take your seats, please.	(d) Sit down, everybody.
5. ___Can you lend me a dime, please?	(e) How do I get to Caesar's?

Answers start on page 50.

Exercise 9

Below is a list of five situations. In the blank in front of each write "formal" if the situation seems to call for formal style and "informal" if the situation seems to call for an informal style.

_____1. You are at a job interview for a job that you really want. You want to seem smart, sensible and cool-headed.

_____2. You are a young man. Five of your best friends drop by your house on a Sunday afternoon to see if you want to go play football in the park.

_____3. You are a 12-year-old in school. You want to ask your teacher for permission to do a short play in front of your class.

_____4. You live in a large city. You have a small daughter who goes to a public school. But the city has decided to shut down the school because there isn't enough money to keep it running. You decide to go to a school board meeting to speak against the school closing.

_____5. You are having dinner, as usual, with your family.

Answers start on page 50.

Using Detailed and General Styles

A **detailed style** is one that gives a lot of very specific information. A writer who uses a detailed style will tell you all the small facts of how something looked or how someone acted. A **general** writer will give you only the broad outline of an event. A general writer gives you the basic idea, without bothering with all the small details. Here are two descriptions of the same party.

1. **Detailed:** I went to a party Janice gave last night. It was at the house of Janice's sister-in-law, June. June is George's wife. George worked for Harold Baker before Harold died. Janice invited Robert, who is her only brother, and his second wife, May. May's sister, Ruth, and her boyfriend, John, came later. She also invited her husband's three sisters. June and Ruth had each bought a new dress for the party, and it turned out to be the same dress—made out of hot pink satin.

2. **General:** I went to Janice's party last night. Mostly family was there. There were quite a few people. The women were all quite dressed up. We had a huge dinner and lots of wine. After dinner, some people danced in the living room. Others drank coffee and talked. The families with young children had to leave first, as the party went on until late.

You can see that writing in a detailed style means that the writer will talk for a long time about a few things. In a general style the writer will cover lots of events in only a few sentences. The writer of the first passage above told us everything we could possibly want to know about the people who came to the party. You can imagine how long it would have taken this writer to tell us about the entire evening! The second writer gave us a general idea of what the whole party was like in only a few lines.

To tell whether a style is general or detailed, think about the events the writer talks about. Ask yourself how much you know about each.

Exercise 10

Read each of the paragraphs below. In the blank after each, write "detailed" or "general," whichever is the style of that paragraph.

I walked by the ocean today. The tide was low. The slope of the beach was very gentle. I could walk way out across sand that had been under water only six hours before. There was some seaweed that had washed in because of a storm at sea. Some of it was very rubbery looking. Plenty of shells lay around. I found mussels, sand dollars, clams and crabs.

1. The style of this passage is _____.

Jack has a thin, bony face. His cheekbones are high and wide. His nose is long, thin and pointy. He is very pale. His hair is red. He lets it grow long. Sometimes it falls almost to his waist. His eyes are pale blue. They are long, narrow eyes that stand out in his face. When he looks at you his eyes are cold and only half-open. The eyelashes and eyebrows are so light in color that you hardly notice them.

2. The style of this passage is _____.

It was a cold morning and I didn't have anywhere to go. It's a working-class neighborhood and almost everyone is at work during the day. I went to a local diner for breakfast. By lunchtime I found myself wandering down Grand Street where the porno shops and penny arcades are. I went home late. My wife was there. We didn't say much to each other.

3.   The style of this passage is _____.

She went to Denver for two days, then moved on to Salt Lake City for three more. She wasn't sure that he was looking for her, but she thought he might be. So, she never stayed in any one place for more than three or four days.

Nights she would be riding, always west, on Greyhound buses. She didn't carry much with her. And later, thinking back, she couldn't remember much about what those days were like.

4.   The style of this passage is _____.

Answers start on page 51.

Looking at Technical and Lyrical Styles

When a writer uses a **technical style,** he or she gives you the plain facts. The writer doesn't give his or her opinion or emotions about the subject. The writer gives you only the details that everyone could agree are true. Scientists write in a technical style. A scientist who writes about rainbows won't tell you that rainbows are pretty or that he likes them. He will give you the plain facts about how and why there are rainbows.

In a **lyrical style** the writer may tell you how he or she feels about the subject. The writer might express an opinion about whether something is good or beautiful or unpleasant.

Exercise 11

Read the passages below and decide whether each is technical or lyrical. Write "technical" or "lyrical" in the blank following the passage.

A human is an animal that walks on two legs. The human is the only animal that speaks. Other animals can make and use tools in a very simple way. For example, some apes will use long sticks to get at things they can't reach with their hands. But the tools that humans make for themselves are much more complex. Humans are mammals. Human babies are born with their eyes open after growing inside the mother for nine months. Humans usually live in families made up of a mother, a father and several children.

1. The style of this passage is _____.

She met him at a party given by a friend. At first she was a little frightened of him. He was older than she was by 15 years. He was successful and well known. He seemed gruff and harsh. He hardly smiled at all. She found as she got to know him that it was one of his many different ways of acting. Two weeks later she knew she was in love with him. It was like a dizzy fall through a long black tunnel. There was no end and no light. There was no way to slow down. There was no way to go back to the past. It was as if the world had closed down into a dark, spinning storm. She couldn't see him straight. He was kind and cold. He told her everything; he told her nothing. He was a snake, a peacock, a fox.

2. The style of this passage is _____.

It was a good winter. I was very happy then. I lived alone that year. I found a tiny apartment on the west side of town. The building was old and drafty, but I liked it there. Every morning I got up before sunrise. The floors were cold and the radiators were just beginning to hum and hiss. There were large windows on the south side of the apartment. At dawn the small rooms took on a golden tinge of sunlight. The bare wood floors and the plain wood rocking chair glowed. The night sky would turn gray, then rose and, finally, a deep, strong blue. There were so many clear days that winter. It hasn't seemed that way since.

3. The style of this passage is _____.

Football is now the most popular American sport. More people watch football games than watch baseball, basketball or tennis. Although football is so well liked in the United States, football is not played in many other countries. Soccer and boxing are the world's most popular sports. Soccer is the favorite sport in most of Europe and South America. Boxing is popular everywhere, especially in Africa. Ice hockey is a favorite sport in some countries that have cold climates like Canada and the Soviet Union.

4. The style of this passage is _____.

Answers start on page 51.

RECOGNIZING TONE

In any writing it is possible to recognize tone. The **tone** of a piece of writing is the general emotion it carries. A piece of writing can be serious, hopeful, amazed, excited, humorous, hopeless, unimpressed, depressed and many other emotions. Any emotion that you can feel can be the tone of a passage.

Let's look at some examples. The first few are labeled for you. For some you will be asked to name the tone.

A certain baseball team took the pennant for the first time in many years. These are the reactions of a few people:

Tone	Statement
Excited	Wow! I can't believe it! This is the best thing that could have happened in this city!
Sentimental	Ah! This is like it was when I was a boy. It makes my chest swell with pride again and brings tears to my eyes.
Serious	The team's manager and coach have had a lot of influence through the season. They deserve a lot of credit for this victory.
Amazed	What!? They won!? And they started off so poorly this season. I just can't believe it!
Sarcastic	It couldn't have been skill since they don't have that. It couldn't have been bribery, since they don't have any money. The other team must all have been sick. It's the only way they could have won.

From this example you can see that different writers will have different responses to the same event. The tone of what each writer says about the baseball team is different.

Exercise 12

In the next five paragraphs you will be given a choice of labels for the tone of each. Choose the word which best describes the tone. Check your answers.

These are the reactions of four people when they heard their friend was arrested for auto theft:

VAL: John has been arrested? I'm afraid he is headed downhill. This is not the first time. Each time it gets worse. I'm worried about him.

1.   The tone of this is
____(1) angry.   ____(3) fearful.   ____(5) sarcastic.
____(2) excited.   ____(4) surprised.

RAY: Go on, John! Soon you'll be able to steal a <u>cookie</u> without your mother knowing it.

2.   The tone of this is
____(1) praising.   ____(3) happy.   ____(5) sentimental.
____(2) sarcastic.   ____(4) hopeful.

ADA: Damn that boy! Won't he ever straighten up?

3.   The tone of this is
____(1) depressed.   ____(3) angry.   ____(5) sarcastic.
____(2) serious.   ____(4) dramatic.

RUTH: He's never been arrested before. Maybe, God willing, this will teach him his lesson. I see a better day coming.

4.   The tone of this is
____(1) hopeful.   ____(3) hopeless.   ____(5) angry.
____(2) sentimental. ____(4) saddened.

DEAN: I showed him just how to do it. He blew it! He could have gotten away with it if he'd just listened to me.

5. The tone of this is

____(1) disappointed.   ____(3) depressed.   ____(5) sarcastic.

____(2) angry.   ____(4) hopeless.

Answers start on page 51.

Exercise 13

Read the following passage. Then choose the best answer. Put a check mark (✔) in front of your choice.

We sat around the fire in the old house. My brothers and I and our father hadn't all been together for a year. It was a cold November day. The four of us sat in the same chairs we sat in the year before. We sat in front of the same fireplace. It seemed like the same fire. Our feelings were almost the same. Only a year had passed. Mother's shawl still hung over the back of her rocker. It had hung there that night a year ago. It hung there on the rocker no one had sat in for a year. It hung there, quietly. It seemed to promise warmth. It hung there just as her memory hung in our minds. We tried to talk, but silence kept breaking in—the silence of the rocker that creaked no more. We four shared the silence of the rocker. We shared the warmth the shawl promised as it lay, like our thoughts, on the rocker.

1. The tone of this passage is

____(1) humorous.   ____(3) hopeless.   ____(5) sarcastic.

____(2) sentimental.   ____(4) angry.

2.   The style of this passage is

___(1) lyrical.   ___(3) general.   ___(5) none of
___(2) formal.   ___(4) technical.   the above

Answers start on page 51.

Exercise 14

Read the passage. Then choose the best answer. Put a check mark ($\checkmark$) in front of your choice.

There have been reports of illness from several families on Route 7 outside the city. The same symptoms have appeared in several people. For this reason, a study has been done. The state health department sent a team of people to find the cause of the disease.

The team sampled the soil for worms. They tested insects for diseases. They checked the foods the sick people had eaten. No clue could be found. Finally, the team found that the water was polluted with animal waste.

This small community does not get its water from the city's water supply. It takes its water from a spring that runs out of a mountain two miles north. At some point the water is being polluted. More studies will be made. For now, all the people are boiling their cooking and drinking water.

1.   This passage sounds most like it came from

_____(1)   a friend gossiping on the telephone.

_____(2)   a news story on the radio.

_____(3)   a letter from a man to a woman.

_____(4)   a public service comic strip in the newspaper.

_____(5)   You can't tell from the passage.

2. The style of the writing is

___(1) detailed.   ___(3) technical.

___(2) formal.   ___(4) all of the above

___(5) none of the above

3. The tone of the passage is

___(1) humorous. ___(3) serious.   ___(5) hopeful.

___(2) angry.   ___(4) depressed.

Answers start on page 52.

Exercise 15

Read this letter. Choose the best answer. Put a check mark
(✔) in front of your choice.

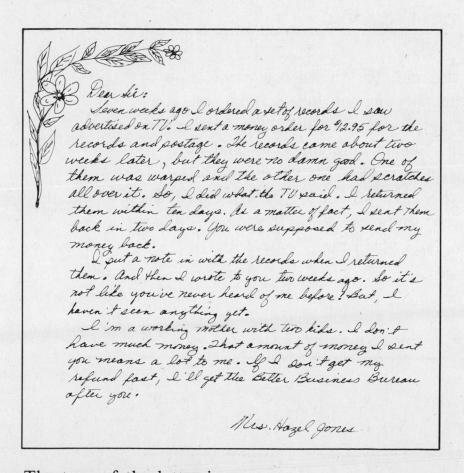

Dear Sir:

Seven weeks ago I ordered a set of records I saw advertised on TV. I sent a money order for $12.95 for the records and postage. The records came about two weeks later, but they were no damn good. One of them was warped and the other one had scratches all over it. So, I did what the TV said. I returned them within ten days. As a matter of fact, I sent them back in two days. You were supposed to send my money back.

I put a note in with the records when I returned them. And then I wrote to you two weeks ago. So it's not like you've never heard of me before! But, I haven't seen anything yet.

I'm a working mother with two kids. I don't have much money. That amount of money I sent you means a lot to me. If I don't get my refund fast, I'll get the Better Business Bureau after you.

Mrs. Hazel Jones

1. The tone of the letter is

___(1) polite.   ___(3) worried.   ___(5) sarcastic.

___(2) angry.   ___(4) hopeful.

2.   The style of the letter is

___(1) formal.   ___(3) lyrical.

___(2) informal.   ___(4) technical.

___(5) none of the above

3.   What is this person likely to do next?

___(1) order more records

___(2) recommend this company to a friend

___(3) call the Better Business Bureau

___(4) sue the record company

___(5) none of the above

Answers start on page 52.

SUMMING UP CRITICAL READING

Your work in this unit has shown you many ways to look at what you read. Sorting out facts and opinions is an important skill. So are seeing a writer's bias and understanding propaganda. Seeing different styles and tones in reading makes it easier to judge what you read.

The exercises you have worked on here are just the beginning. Try to keep using these skills. In your day-to-day life, there are many times you'll need to be critical.

REVIEW EXERCISE—CRITICAL READING

Review Exercise 1

Read this ad. Listen for the writer's purpose, style and tone. Then answer the questions that follow.

Got a date tonight? Want to look your very best? Don't forget, the best-dressed woman is wearing a smile, and you won't smile your best unless you remember your Get Close Toothpaste. Only Get Close has the special blend of cleaners and whiteners that will make your smile really sparkle. Even if you're a woman who smokes, Get Close will give you a smile that is dazzlingly white. A smile he won't be able to resist. Dull teeth make a dull smile. And a dull smile will mean a dull date. Don't take any chances. There's only one toothpaste that guarantees that he'll want to get close.

1. List three loaded words or phrases that are meant to cause a powerful, positive feeling in women.

    (a) _____

    (b) _____

    (c) _____

2. What loaded word is used over and over to give a bad feeling?

    _____

3. The writer's purpose here is to
    _____(1)   get more women to brush regularly.
    _____(2)   show the purpose of sparkling teeth.
    _____(3)   sell Get Close Toothpaste to more women.
    _____(4)   help people look better.
    _____(5)   help people get more dates.

4. What is the tone of the ad?
    _____(1)   excited
    _____(2)   fearful
    _____(3)   hopeless
    _____(4)   sarcastic
    _____(5)   sentimental

5. Which of the following is a fact and not an opinion?
    _____(1)   There's only one toothpaste that guarantees that he'll want to get close.
    _____(2)   You'll have a smile he won't be able to resist.
    _____(3)   A dull smile will mean a dull date.
    _____(4)   The best-dressed woman is wearing a smile.
    _____(5)   none of the above

ANSWERS AND EXPLANATIONS—CRITICAL READING

Exercise 1

1. Fact. Weather records can be checked.
2. Opinion. Different people have different opinions about this.
3. Opinion. This cannot be proved. It is the opinion of the speaker.
4. Fact. By weighing each one, this can be proved.
5. Fact. Checking pay records can prove this.

Exercise 2

1. We were told that the writer is telling the truth. These sentences are the only ones that we could check and prove to be true:

    (6)   It is now true that half of all marriages end in divorce.
    (7)   For every two weddings there will be one divorce.
    (8)   Further, the rate of divorce is climbing.
    (9)   Only ten years ago, the divorce rate was one out of three.
    (10) Now it is one out of two.

2. (2) A stable way of life in America can only be based on stable families.
    (3) Divorce causes our world to weaken.

    These are the only two sentences that show the writer's bias or opinion. (1) and (5) are facts. (4) is not what this writer believes.

3. (1)   Yes, the writer sounds worried about the world.

Exercise 3

1. (2)   Prostitution is rarely legal. In the U.S. only the state of Nevada allows prostitution. It would be hard to prove (1), (3), (4) and (5).
2. (2)   prostitution should be made legal because it would be better for most people involved. The writer gave several ideas to support this opinion.
3. (3)   Only women can be prostitutes. The writer gives us information about men in the profession, too. (1), (2), (4) and (5) are statements of the writer's opinion.

Exercise 4

1. (5)   One-third of the children in America watch TV for an average of six hours everyday. We could look up the figures on this statement or look at the way the writer came up with the statement. We could prove it to be true or false. (1), (2), (3) and (4) are statements of the writer's opinions about TV.
2. (3)   Time watching TV could be better spent doing other things. The writer is totally against children watching TV. He feels they should be out playing or reading.
3. (1)   playing outside. The writer says a child's hours are better spent playing outside or reading a book.

Exercise 5

1. Bad.   The first sentence is supposed to have a bad effect on the reader. The loaded words are

ragged, smelly, tramp and shack. Unloaded, the sentence could have been, "The man died of exposure."

2. Bad.   This sentence also has a bad effect. The loaded words are blew up, storm and angry. Unloaded, the sentence could have been, "The meeting ended without reaching agreement."

3. Good.   This sentence is loaded in a pleasant way. The loaded words are pride and joy and talented. Unloaded, the sentence could have been, "Miss Davis won the dance contest.

4. Bad.   This sentence has a bad effect. The loaded words are dirty, dreary and rundown.

5. Good.   This sentence has two pleasantly loaded words: bright and sparkling.

6. Bad.   There are four unpleasantly loaded words in this sentence: angry, mob, hissed and booed.

7. Good.   This sentence has a good effect. The loaded words are vision of loveliness.

8. Good.   In this pleasantly loaded sentence you should have underlined trim, tidy and neat.

9. Bad.   This sentence has an unpleasant effect. The loaded words are terrible, force, blast and hurled.

10. Bad.   The effect of this sentence is unpleasant. The loaded words are slob and filthy.

Exercise 6

1. (3)   fear of losing someone important. The ad tries to play on a woman's fear of losing her husband.
2. You should have chosen three of these words or phrases:
   (a) dingy
   (b) dirty

(c) grime

(d) you don't care about him anymore

(e) not as beautiful

(f) something is wrong

3. You should have chosen three of these words or phrases:

(a) gentle   (d) renew

(b) you care   (e) brightness

(c) loving   (f) warmth

Exercise 7

1. (3) Smoking is dangerous to health. The first sentence says that doctors found smoking <u>is</u> dangerous. The writer doesn't argue with that at all. All the examples show that he agrees.

2. (2) negative; all the words are used to make people stop smoking.

3. (2) stop signs; the last sentence of the passage does this.

4. (4) They could seriously endanger their lives.

Exercise 8

1. (c)

2. (e)

3. (b)

4. (d)

5. (a)

Exercise 9

1. formal

2. informal

3. formal
4. formal
5. informal

Exercise 10

1. The style of this passage is <u>detailed</u>.
2. The style of this passage is <u>detailed</u>.
3. The style of this passage is <u>general</u>.
4. The style of this passage is <u>general</u>.

Exercise 11

1. The style of this passage is <u>technical</u>.
2. The style of this passage is <u>lyrical</u>.
3. The style of this passage is <u>lyrical</u>.
4. The style of this passage is <u>technical</u>.

Exercise 12

1. Val: (3) fearful.
2. Ray: (2) sarcastic.
3. Ada: (3) angry.
4. Ruth: (1) hopeful.
5. Dean: (1) disappointed. Or (2) angry.

Exercise 13

1. (2) sentimental
2. (1) lyrical

Exercise 14

1. (2) a news story on the radio.
2. (4) all of the above.
3. (3) serious.

Exercise 15

1. (2) angry
2. (2) informal
3. (3) call the Better Business Bureau

ANSWERS AND EXPLANATIONS—REVIEW EXERCISE

Review Exercise 1

1. You might have listed three of these:
    (a)   sparkle
    (b)   the best-dressed woman
    (c)   dazzlingly white
    (d)   special blend
    (e)   guarantees
2. dull, dull, dull
3. (3)   Sell Get Close Toothpaste to more women. Most
          ads are not written to help people. The purpose is
          to get more people to buy the product.
4. (1)   excited; the passage tries to excite women enough
          so they will want to buy the toothpaste.
5. (5)   none of the above; all of the statements are
          propaganda.

2 | PRACTICAL READING: FOLLOW-ING WRITTEN DIRECTIONS

How many times have things like these happened to you?

- You stop at a gas station to get directions. You listen and try to remember everything. By the time the person tells you to turn right after the third stoplight five miles down the road, you are lost.

- You decide to try a do-it-yourself project in your home or on your car. When you think you are finished, you have parts left over. The project does not look as good as you thought it would. It doesn't work right, either.

- You are trying a new recipe. You hope that it turns out all right. It doesn't and no one wants to eat it. You end up throwing the whole thing away. You vow never to cook from a recipe again.

Why do things like these seem to happen at times to all of us? Following directions someone <u>tells</u> you isn't easy. Following <u>written</u> directions is even harder. There is no one secret to make following directions easy. It takes practice.

Here are some rules that can help you get better at working with written directions.

1. Read everything first.
2. Find a place to start.

3. Make sure you understand any symbols or illustrations used.
4. Divide the directions into steps.
5. Have all the materials you will need handy.
6. Picture in your mind how you will follow each step.

Here is a set of written directions for getting to Baum's Discount Store from Holloway's Gas Station on 24th Street. Read everything first. Then go back and read the directions again. Look for a place to start. Picture yourself going from there. Follow the directions in your mind. We are going to draw a map from these directions, but first, do the reading.

To get to Baum's Discount Store from Holloway's Gas Station, you go north three blocks on 24th Street until you come to the stoplight. This is Grand Avenue.

Make a left turn onto Grand Avenue. Go west on Grand, crossing 23rd Street, 22nd Street and 21st Street. When you come to 20th Street, make a right turn. You'll be heading north. Go north on 20th Street. Cross over Lee Avenue. Watch for the library on your left. The next corner is 20th and Main.

Baum's Discount Store is right next to the library on the southwest corner of 20th and Main.

Use a blank piece of paper and follow along as we go.

Where is the starting place? Holloway's Gas Station at 24th Street. Which direction are you to travel on 24th

Street? North. In drawing maps, put the compass points in one corner. This will help keep your directions and turns clear. The compass points look like this:

Imagine that you are part of the instructions, not just a listener. Put yourself right on 24th Street by the gas station ready to drive or walk north. Start at the lower right-hand corner of your paper. Draw the start of the map like this:

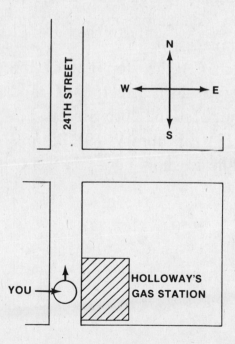

Now drawing the rest of the map will not be too hard. You're headed in the right direction on 24th Street. You go three blocks north to the stoplight.

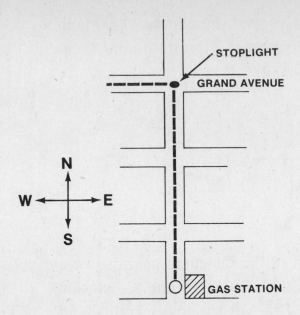

Go back to the directions. Try to finish the map and get all the way to Baum's Discount Store. Check your map with the one that follows to see how you came out. On your drawing, label all the following places:

(1) Holloway's Gas Station; (2) the stoplight at the corner of Grand and 24th Street; (3) 24th Street; (4) Grand Avenue; (5) 23rd Street; (6) 22nd, 21st and 20th Streets; (7) Lee Avenue and Main Street; (8) the library; (9) Baum's Discount Store. Use a dotted line to show how you went.

Your drawing doesn't have to be fancy. This one isn't.
Does your map come close to this one?

GOING TO BAUM'S DISCOUNT STORE
FROM HOLLOWAY'S GAS STATION

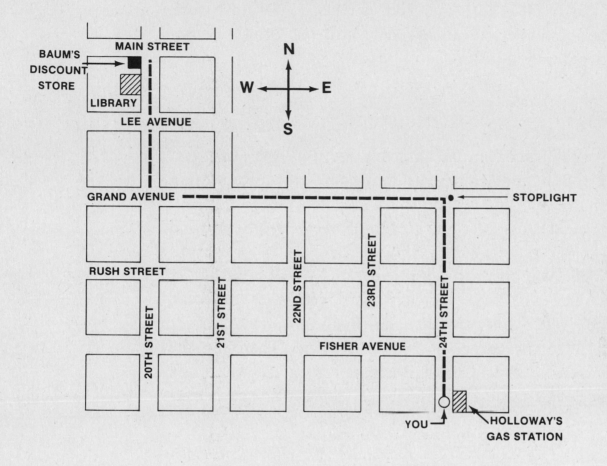

After the left turn onto Grand Avenue, did you cross
23rd, 22nd and 21st to get onto 20th? Did the right turn
cause you any trouble? And how about the southwest corner
of 20th and Main?

If you were off a little, don't worry. In this unit there is
good practice for following all kinds of directions.

Exercise 1

Read the following directions. Then draw the map. You may use the one you just worked on. Label the following streets and places: (1) Baum's Discount Store; (2) 20th, 21st, 22nd, 23rd, 24th, 25th and 26th Streets; (3) Main Street, Sherman Avenue and Jones Boulevard; (4) Crown Recreation Center.

To get from Baum's Discount Store on the southwest corner of 20th and Main Street to the new Crown Recreation Center is easy. All you do is go five blocks east on Main Street. You cross 21st Street, 22nd Street, 23rd Street and 24th.

When you come to 25th Street and Main, turn left or north. Go two blocks north. You'll pass over Sherman Avenue. When you come to Jones Boulevard, make a right turn. Go to the corner of 26th and Jones. There, on the southeast corner, is Crown Recreation Center. The main entrance to Crown is right at 26th and Jones. You can't miss it.

Answers start on page 88.

Exercise 2

In the next exercise, you will draw a map from a description of the inside of the Crown Recreation Center. The skills you used to draw the other maps will help you follow the directions in this exercise.

Remember to find a starting place. Use the diagram that follows. Draw and label everything that is underlined in the description.

CROWN RECREATION CENTER

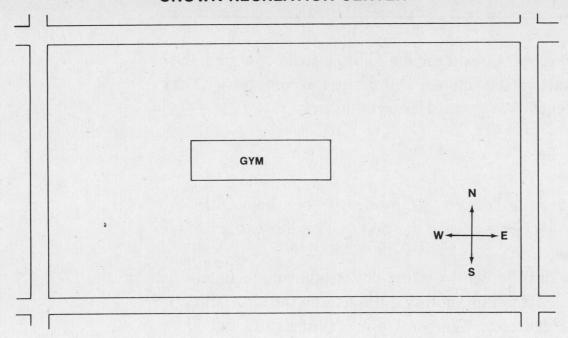

The Crown Recreation Center covers almost a whole city block. Twenty-sixth Street is on the west side of the Center. On the east is 27th Street. Jones Boulevard runs along the north and Sherman Avenue along the south.

In the middle of the Crown Center is the gym. Right next to the gym on the east are the handball courts. Right next to the gym on the west is the swimming pool.

North of the gym are the outdoor basketball courts. North of the courts along Jones Boulevard is a grassy picnic area.

In the northeast corner of Crown Center is the kiddie playground with slides, swings, merry-go-round, etc. South of the kiddie area is another picnic area.

There is an entrance in the southeast corner of Crown. Just west of this entrance is a football field. And in the southwest corner is a baseball diamond and another entrance. There is a third entrance in the northwest corner of the center.

Answers start on page 88.

Exercise 3

In this exercise, you will draw a figure instead of a map. Use all the hints in the following directions as you did with the maps. Remember to read everything first.

Draw a circle that fits inside the box below. In the center of this circle place a dot that you can see easily. Mark this dot with a 1.

Now draw a line from the dot straight up to touch the top of the circle. Put another dot touching the circle directly below the center or number 1 dot. Number this dot 2.

Place a third dot on the circle about ½ inch to the left of dot 2. Number this one 3. Now put a fourth dot on the circle about ½ inch to the right of dot number 2. This dot is number 4.

Go back to dot 1 in the center of the circle. Draw a line from this dot to dot number 3, to the left on the circle. Do the same thing to dot number 4, on the right. Do not draw any line to the second dot.

As you know, following directions applies to many different things. Besides telling you how to get to different places, directions can also be given for making things. You can sew a skirt, build a dollhouse, bake a cake or make a model airplane from written directions. Written directions can also show you how to do things. The instructions you will work on next are different from the ones you've read so far. In some you will be looking at diagrams that are part of the directions. In others you will simply read and then answer questions about them. In the map drawing exercise at the beginning of this unit, there were six important rules for following directions. We'll repeat them here:

1. Read everything first.
2. Find a starting point.
3. Make sure you understand any symbols or illustrations used.
4. Divide the directions into steps.
5. Have all the materials you will need handy.
6. Picture in your mind how you will follow each step.

Answers start on page 89.

Exercise 4

Read the directions for dancing the Country Swing. Study the diagram. Try the steps with a partner. Then answer the questions that follow.

MAN'S PART

WOMAN'S PART

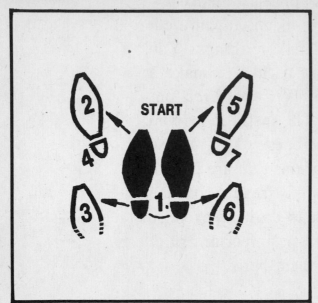

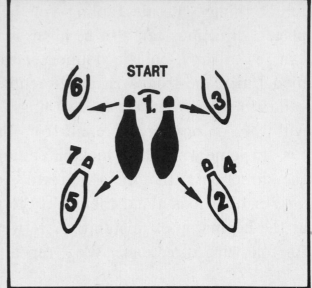

The Country Swing

These are the steps for the man's part. The woman's part is the exact opposite. She does steps 5-7 when he does 2-4. The two partners face each other.

1. Start with feet together. This is the closed position.

2. Take your left foot and step to the side slightly.

3. Put the ball of your right foot behind your left foot. Shift your weight to the right foot.

4. Replace your weight quickly onto your left foot.

5. Using your right foot, take a small step to the side.

6. Place the ball of your left foot behind your right. Shift your weight to the left foot.

7. Replace your weight quickly onto the right.

1. Where are your feet when you start the country swing?
   _____(1) in a closed position, left foot in front
   _____(2) in a closed position, right foot in front
   _____(3) feet together, toes pointing out

_____(4)   in a closed position with feet together

_____(5)   feet together, toes pointing in

2. What is the difference betweeen the man's and the woman's part?

_____(1)   no difference

_____(2)   She steps right when he steps left.

_____(3)   She steps left when he steps back.

_____(4)   She steps back when he steps right.

_____(5)   She keeps both feet together when he steps left slightly.

3. In the man's position where should his left foot be in Step 3?

_____(1)   slightly to the left side in front of the right foot

_____(2)   slightly to the right side in front of the right foot

_____(3)   behind the right foot slightly to the left

_____(4)   alongside the right foot

_____(5)   pointing in

4. In the woman's position where should her left foot be when the man is doing Step 7?

_____(1)   behind her right foot

_____(2)   next to her right foot

_____(3)   directly opposite, but next to the man's right foot

_____(4)   directly in front of the man's right foot

_____(5)   next to her own right foot

5. What step should the woman be doing when the man is doing step 4?

_____(1)   step 3

_____(2)   step 4

_____(3)　step 5

_____(4)　step 6

_____(5)　step 7

Answers start on page 89.

Exercise 5

Here is an easy, fun project you can do for yourself or as a gift for a friend. This exercise gives step-by-step directions for putting a pretty paper or cloth cover on a soft-cover or paperback book. All you need is cardboard, a piece of paper or cloth, white glue and a few other things. Read all the directions to find out more about how the project works. Try it if you like or just picture yourself following each step. Study the drawings carefully as you read the directions. Then answer the questions that follow.

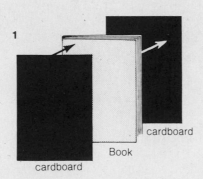

1.　Cut the cardboard into two pieces. Each should be the size of the front or back cover of the book. Glue one piece of cardboard on the back and the other piece on the front of the book. Let this dry under a stack of books for 20 minutes. See drawing 1.

2.　Cut the paper or cloth fabric large enough to cover the front, back and spine of the book. Allow an extra ¾ of an inch on all four sides. In pencil trace the outline of the book on the wrong side of the paper. (The wrong side is the side of the paper that won't show when the cover is on the book.) Place the paper so that the two longest sides are at the top and bottom. Draw a line down the center of the paper. Then draw a pencil line around the spine of the book.

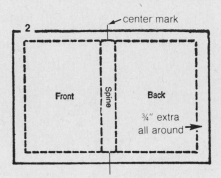

Place the book open with spine down on the center of the paper so that the center of the spine lines up with the line you have just drawn. See drawing 2.

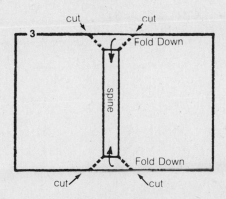
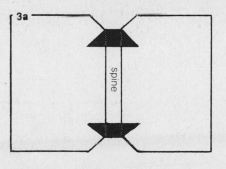

3. Remove the book. Cut along the dotted lines as shown in drawing 3. Fold the flaps inward and glue them down as shown in drawing 3a.

4. Put glue on the outside of the spine of the book. Press the paper against it until the glue is dry. (About 15-20 minutes) Then glue the paper to

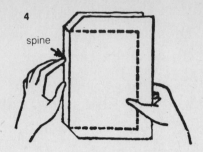

the front and back covers of the closed book.
See drawing 4. Let this dry 15-20 minutes.

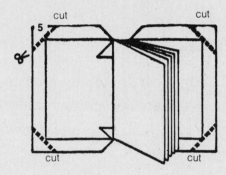

5. Open the book and cut the four corners as
shown in drawing 5.

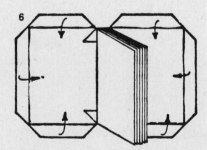

6. Fold over the edges and glue them down to the
inside of the covers of the book as shown in
drawing 6. Let these dry 15-20 minutes.

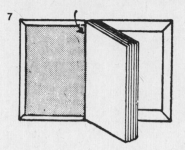

7. Close the book. Measure the front cover. Cut two more pieces of paper or cloth the size of the front cover. Cut ¼ inch off the long side and ½ inch off the shorter side of each piece. Glue these to the inside of the cover you have just pasted on the book. See drawing 7. Let these dry 15-20 minutes.

1. Which of the following sets of materials lists something you do NOT need for this project?
    _____(1)   glue, scissors, pencil, cardboard
    _____(2)   glue, string, pencil, cardboard
    _____(3)   glue, paper or cloth, pencil, cardboard
    _____(4)   glue, stack of books, pencil, cardboard
    _____(5)   pencil, scissors, paper or cloth, glue

2. Picture yourself doing each step of these directions. About how much time should it take you to finish?
    _____(1)   You can't tell from the directions.
    _____(2)   about 20 minutes
    _____(3)   about 1 day
    _____(4)   about 2 hours
    _____(5)   about 2 days

3. When do you glue on the first piece of cardboard?

_____(1) during step 1

_____(2) during step 2

_____(3) during step 3

_____(4) during step 4

_____(5) during step 5

4. What kind of book could you use for this project?

_____(1) a large hard-back dictionary

_____(2) a small hard-back dictionary

_____(3) a big magazine

_____(4) any kind of book will work

_____(5) None of the above will work.

5. What kind of glue should you use?

_____(1) rubber cement

_____(2) contact cement

_____(3) quick-drying glue

_____(4) waterproof glue

_____(5) white glue

6. Which of the following is NOT something you do in this project?

_____(1) fold down two flaps

_____(2) tie the paper to the book

_____(3) cut two pieces of cardboard

_____(4) cut two pieces of paper

_____(5) cut off four corners of the paper

Answers start on page 89.

A **recipe** is a list of directions for making something to eat or drink. Often the recipe will start with a list of everything you will need. Some recipes will tell you how

much of the food you will make. This is called the **yield.**
The next exercise is a recipe for something delicious.

Exercise 6

Read this recipe for Fat Fanny's Fudge from Florida. Study all the parts of the recipe. Imagine yourself following the directions. Answer the questions that follow.

FAT FANNY'S FUDGE   *Yields about*
FROM FLORIDA   *1 ½ pounds*

2 squares unsweetened chocolate, shaved
2 cups sugar
1½ tablespoons corn syrup
¾ cup light cream
½ teaspoon salt
2 tablespoons butter
1 teaspoon vanilla extract

In heavy, medium-size saucepan, combine chocolate, sugar, corn syrup, cream and salt. Place over low heat and stir until chocolate has melted. Bring to a boil over low heat and continue cooking—without stirring—until a drop of chocolate in cold water forms a soft ball—about 15 minutes. Remove from heat and place butter on top—do not stir. Let stand until lukewarm. Add vanilla and stir with wooden spoon until thick or until fudge just begins to lose its gloss. Lightly butter inside of small square pan and add fudge. Refrigerate to set—about ½ hour—and cut into squares.

Reprinted from *Cooking Up a Storm* by Sidney P. Waud.

1. How many different ingredients does this recipe call for?
    _____(1)   five
    _____(2)   ten
    _____(3)   eight
    _____(4)   seven
    _____(5)   six

2. Which of these would <u>not</u> be needed to make Fat Fanny's Fudge?
    _____(1)   a saucepan
    _____(2)   butter
    _____(3)   a wooden spoon
    _____(4)   a small square pan
    _____(5)   a candy thermometer

3. How do you know when you've boiled the chocolate long enough?
    _____(1)   when the top is covered with bubbles
    _____(2)   when foam forms on the top
    _____(3)   when the chocolate loses its gloss
    _____(4)   when the chocolate moves from the sides of the pan
    _____(5)   when a drop of the chocolate forms a soft ball when it is dropped into cold water

4. Which of these should you have a little extra of to make Fat Fanny's Fudge?
    _____(1)   chocolate
    _____(2)   butter
    _____(3)   corn syrup
    _____(4)   light cream
    _____(5)   sugar

5. How much fudge will this recipe make?

_____(1)   1½ squares

_____(2)   2 pounds

_____(3)   1½ pounds

_____(4)   It depends on how big you cut the squares.

_____(5)   12 squares

6. Fill in the missing steps needed to make Fat Fanny's Fudge.

(1)   In the saucepan mix together the chocolate, sugar, corn syrup, cream and salt.

(2)   Place over low heat and stir until chocolate has melted.

(3)   _____

_____

_____

(4)   Remove from heat and place butter on top. Do not stir.

(5)   _____

_____

_____

(6)   Add vanilla and stir until thick or until fudge just begins to lose its gloss.

(7)   _____

_____

_____

(8)   Refrigerate to set (about ½ hour).

(9)   _____

_____

_____

Answers start on page 90.

Exercise 7

Read the directions for this stomach-trimming workout. Study the picture. Then answer the questions that follow.

TRIM YOUR STOMACH

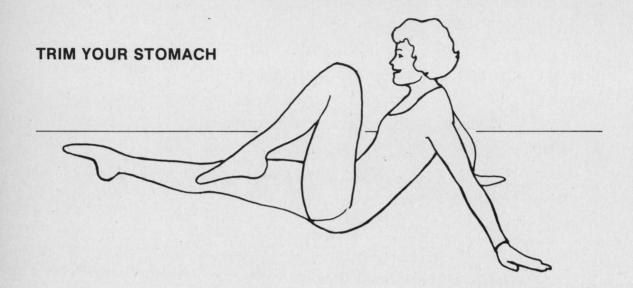

Sit down on the floor with both legs out in front of you. Lean back a little, and place your hands on the floor behind you. Keep your elbows straight. Bend your left knee and pull it up to your stomach. Keep your left leg out straight in front of you, but lift it off the floor. Now bend your right knee up to your stomach. Straighten out your left leg in front of you. Always straighten one leg as you pull in the other. Your feet should stay off the floor. Do this five times with each leg. If you do this each day, it is a good way to trim your waist and build strong stomach muscles.

1. How many times should you repeat this exercise?
   _____(1)   as many times as you can
   _____(2)   ten times all together
   _____(3)   five times for the left leg only
   _____(4)   once a week
   _____(5)   five times a day

2. What is the purpose of this exercise?

_____(1) It flattens the bust.

_____(2) It strengthens the back.

_____(3) It reduces strain.

_____(4) It trims the waist.

_____(5) It builds the arm muscles.

3. Where should the feet be during the exercise?

_____(1) They should stay flat on the floor.

_____(2) They should stay off the floor.

_____(3) The left foot should always stay on the floor.

_____(4) Only the right leg should touch the floor.

_____(5) none of the above

4. How often should you do this exercise?

_____(1) five times a day

_____(2) five times a week

_____(3) seven times a week

_____(4) once a week

_____(5) once a month

5. Where should your left leg be when your right knee is pulled up to your stomach?

_____(1) straight out in front of you, on the floor

_____(2) pulled in just like your right knee

_____(3) out to the side

_____(4) straight out in front of you, off the floor

_____(5) none of the above

6. Rewrite the directions for the exercise in numbered steps. Use as many steps as you think are needed. Use a blank space of paper.

Answers start on page 91.

Exercise 8

Directions for filling out forms are often written as you see them on this application for employment. Study the form. Notice that parts of the form are labeled A, B, C, D and E. The questions that follow ask you to imagine that this application is being filled out by a person named Joe Simpson. Joe is applying for a job at Anderson's Hardware Company.

APPLICATION FOR EMPLOYMENT

PERSONAL INFORMATION

Date   Social Security Number

Name   Age   Sex

    Last   First   Middle

Present Address

    Street   City   State   Zip

(C) Permanent Address

    Street   City   State   Zip

Phone Number   Own Home   Rent   Board   **(A)**

Date of Birth   Height   Weight   Color of Hair   Color of Eyes

Married   Single   Widowed   Divorced   Separated

Number of Children   **(E)** Dependents Other Than Wife or Children   Citizen of U. S. A.   Yes O   No O

(B) If Related to Anyone in Our Employ, State Name and Department   Referred By

EMPLOYMENT DESIRED

Position   Date You Can Start   Salary Desired

Are You Employed Now?   If So May We Inquire of Your Present Employer

(D) Ever Applied to this Company Before?   Where   When

(Side labels: Last, First, Middle)

1. Joe Simpson is going to move soon. He wants all of his mail to go to his parents' house. Where should he write their address on the form?

    _____(1)   Part A

    _____(2)   Part B

    _____(3)   Part C

_____(4)   Part D

_____(5)   Part E

2. Joe lives in an apartment building. Where should he show this?

_____(1)   Part A

_____(2)   Part B

_____(3)   Part C

_____(4)   Part D

_____(5)   Part E

3. Joe is applying for a job at Anderson's Hardware Company. Four years ago he applied for a job there but did not get it. Where should he show this?

_____(1)   Part A

_____(2)   Part B

_____(3)   Part C

_____(4)   Part D

_____(5)   Part E

4. Joe gives part of his money to his parents who are retired. Where should he show this?

_____(1)   Part A

_____(2)   Part B

_____(3)   Part C

_____(4)   Part D

_____(5)   Part E

5. Joe's uncle is a foreman at this company. Where should he show this?

_____(1)   Part A

_____(2)   Part B

_____(3)   Part C

_____(4)   Part D

_____(5)   Part E

Answers start on page 91.

Exercise 9

Read the following directions for writing checks. Look at the sample check that follows. Parts are labeled (a), (b), (c), (d), (e) and (f). Then fill out the three blank checks. Make out each check for the amount of money shown above it. Also fill out the check stubs. You may use the name Ann Smith to sign each check. Use the date July 10, 1981.

(f)

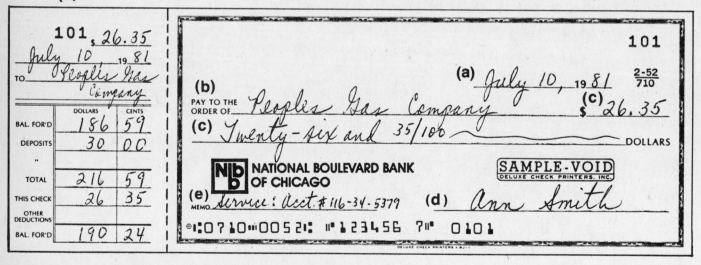

(a) Date

In writing the check, the date should be today's date. Dating a check for some time in the future (when you plan to have enough money in the bank to cover the check) should never be done and is illegal in some cases. For this exercise use the date July 10, 1981.

(b) Pay to the Order of

A check made out to cash will not serve as a receipt and can be cashed by anyone if it is lost. Therefore, you should always make out the check to "Pay to the order of" the person or company you wish to pay.

(c) Amount

The amount of the check is written in figures just next to the dollar sign. The same amount is then written in words on the line below, starting at the far left. Any part less than a dollar is put over 100. A straight or wavy line is used to fill in the unused part of the line. In this way the amount of money cannot be changed.

(d) Signature

The signature is the same name, same initials and same style of writing that were used on the signature card. Use the name Ann Smith for this exercise.

(e) Memo

This space can be used to briefly state the purpose of the check. The space may be used to note anything important about the check.

(f) Check Stub

It is very important to fill out the check stub and figure your new balance right after making out the check.

1. $34.02 to High Value Food Store for groceries. The account has a balance of $100.00 before this check is written.

103 $_____

_____19____

TO_____

	DOLLARS	CENTS
BAL. FOR'D		
DEPOSITS		
''		
TOTAL		
THIS CHECK		
OTHER DEDUCTIONS		
BAL. FOR'D		

103

_____19____   2-52 / 710

PAY TO THE ORDER OF_____ $_____

_____ DOLLARS

NATIONAL BOULEVARD BANK OF CHICAGO

SAMPLE-VOID
DELUXE CHECK PRINTERS, INC.

MEMO_____

⑆0710⑈0052⑆ ⑈123456 7⑈ 0153

2. $132.00 to Gale's Fashion Clothes for a winter coat. The account has a balance of $340.00 before the check is written.

104 $_____

_____19____

TO_____

	DOLLARS	CENTS
BAL. FOR'D		
DEPOSITS		
''		
TOTAL		
THIS CHECK		
OTHER DEDUCTIONS		
BAL. FOR'D		

104

_____19____   2-52 / 710

PAY TO THE ORDER OF_____ $_____

_____ DOLLARS

NATIONAL BOULEVARD BANK OF CHICAGO

SAMPLE-VOID
DELUXE CHECK PRINTERS, INC.

MEMO_____

⑆0710⑈0052⑆ ⑈123456 7⑈ 0154

3. $251.35 to the Valley Center Department Store. The account has a balance of $400.00 before the check is written.

Answers start on page 92.

REVIEW EXERCISES—PRACTICAL READING: FOLLOWING DIRECTIONS

Review Exercise 1

Read this recipe for Pumpkin Squares. Then answer the questions that follow.

Pumpkin Squares

Grease the bottom of a 13 by 9-inch pan. To make the crust, combine a package of yellow cake mix with an egg and a half cup of melted margarine. Save one cup of this for the topping. Press the rest into the pan. Put three cups of pumpkin-pie filling, 2 eggs and ⅔ cup of milk in a bowl. Mix until smooth. Pour this mixture over the crust (in the pan). To make the topping, mix together the remaining cup of the cake-egg-margarine mixture, ¼ cup of sugar, ¼ cup of soft margarine and a teaspoon of cinnamon. Sprinkle this over the mixture in the pan. Bake at 350° for 45-55 minutes. Serves 15 people.

1. In what order do you make the three parts of the Pumpkin Squares?
   _____(1)   topping, filling, crust
   _____(2)   crust, topping, filling
   _____(3)   crust, filling, topping
   _____(4)   filling, crust, topping
   _____(5)   topping, crust, filling

2. How much margarine do you need to make Pumpkin Squares?
   _____(1)   1 cup melted and 1 cup soft
   _____(2)   ½ cup melted and ¼ cup soft

_____(3)　¼ cup melted and ½ cup soft

_____(4)　½ cup melted

_____(5)　¼ cup soft

3.　How many eggs do you need to make Pumpkin Squares?

_____(1)　1 egg

_____(2)　2 eggs

_____(3)　3 eggs

_____(4)　4 eggs

_____(5)　none

4.　How many people does this recipe serve?

_____(1)　15 people

_____(2)　 5 people

_____(3)　45 people

_____(4)　5 to 10 people

_____(5)　You can't tell from the recipe.

5.　How do you cook the recipe?

_____(1)　It doesn't have to be cooked.

_____(2)　You bake it at 500° for 45-55 minutes.

_____(3)　You bake it at 350° for 15 minutes.

_____(4)　You bake it at 350° for one hour.

_____(5)　You bake it at 350° for 45-55 minutes.

Answers start on page 93.

Review Exercise 2

Read the instructions and study the picture for doing the Three-Leaf Clover with a yo-yo. Then answer the questions that follow.

Three-Leaf-Clover

Throw the yo-yo out in front of you, but slightly upward. This first motion is known as *Forward Pass*. As the yo-yo comes back toward you, flick your wrist inward and throw the yo-yo out directly in front of you again. You should make a loop and one of the clovers. When the yo-yo comes back to you a second time, flick your wrist so that the yo-yo goes inside your arm and moves downward toward the floor; that's the stem of your clover. Then jerk your wrist to make the yo-yo come back up to your hand.

Mr. Yo-Yo™ Duncan® diagram from *The Art of Yo-Yo Playing*, copyright 1950, Donald F. Duncan. Used by permission of Flambeau Products Corp.

1. How many steps are there in the directions?

    _____(1) three steps

    _____(2) four steps

    _____(3) five steps

    _____(4) six steps

    _____(5) seven steps

2. What is the last movement of your wrist when you do this trick?

    _____(1) Flick your wrist inward.

    _____(2) Flick your wrist outward.

_____(3) Jerk your wrist to make the yo-yo come back to your hand.

_____(4) Jerk your wrist so the yo-yo goes inside your arm.

_____(5) Flick your wrist so the yo-yo goes outside your arm.

3. When the yo-yo comes back to you the second time, what do you do?

_____(1) Flick your wrist inward and throw the yo-yo.

_____(2) Throw the yo-yo out in front of you.

_____(3) Flick your wrist so the yo-yo goes inside your arm and down.

_____(4) Flick your wrist so the yo-yo goes outside your arm and down.

_____(5) Jerk your wrist to make the yo-yo come back up to your hand.

4. A Forward Pass is done by

_____(1) Flicking your wrist.

_____(2) Jerking your wrist slightly upward.

_____(3) Jerking your wrist slightly downward.

_____(4) Throwing the yo-yo out in front of you, slightly upward.

_____(5) Throwing the yo-yo out in front of you, slightly downward.

5. Where is the yo-yo when you finish the Three-Leaf-Clover?

_____(1) near the floor

_____(2)   in your hand

_____(3)   straight behind you

_____(4)   straight in front of you

_____(5)   The directions don't say.

Answers start on page 93.

Review Exercise 3

Follow these directions to make a drawing. Then guess what it is you have drawn.

Draw a dot in the middle of a piece of paper. Under the dot, write the letter H. Draw another dot straight north of the first one, about two inches away. Above this dot write the number 2. Midway between these dots, make a third dot. Draw a small square around this dot. Place the letter P above it. About one inch straight west of this P square, draw another dot with a 3 under it. One inch directly east of the P square, draw another dot with a 1 under it. Connect the dots with straight lines going from H to 1 to 2 to 3 and back to H again. What figure have you drawn?

Answers start on page 93.

Review Exercise 4

Jan Harris is going to apply for a charge card. She has to fill out a form like the one shown on the next page. Note that parts of the Charge Card Request are labeled A,B,C,D,E, and F. Use these to answer the questions.

Charge Card Request

(BANK USE ONLY)

CL	
CDS	

(A)

| LAST NAME | MIDDLE | FIRST NAME | SOCIAL SECURITY NO. | BIRTHDATE |

| PRESENT STREET ADDRESS | | YEARS THERE | OWN ☐ RENT ☐ | RENTAL PAYMENT MORTGAGE PAYMENT $ |

| CITY | STATE | ZIP | AREA CODE TELEPHONE NUMBER ( ) | NUMBER OF DEPENDENTS | **(D)** |

(F) | PREVIOUS STREET ADDRESS (IF LESS THAN 3 YEARS AT PRESENT ADDRESS) | CITY | STATE | ZIP | YEARS THERE |

(E) | NAME OF NEAREST RELATIVE NOT LIVING WITH YOU | RELATIONSHIP |

| ADDRESS | CITY | STATE | AREA CODE TELEPHONE NUMBER ( ) |

| PRESENT EMPLOYER | POSITION OR TITLE | AREA CODE TELEPHONE NUMBER ( ) |

| ADDRESS | CITY | STATE | ZIP | YEARS THERE |

(C) | PREVIOUS EMPLOYER | YEARS THERE | AREA CODE TELEPHONE NUMBER ( ) |

| ADDRESS | CITY | STATE |

ALIMONY, CHILD SUPPORT, OR SEPARATE MAINTENANCE PAYMENTS SHOULD NOT BE LISTED.

| PRESENT MONTHLY NET SALARY $ | OTHER INCOME $ | PER MO. ☐ YR. ☐ | SOURCE OF OTHER INCOME: | **(B)** |

1. Jan lives with her mother, sister and her four children. Her brother lives in another town. Her best friend lives next door. Whose name should she write in part E?

_____(1) her best friend's name

_____(2) her brother's name

_____(3) her sister's name

_____(4) her mother's name

_____(5) her oldest son's name

2. Jan has four children. Where should she write this information?

_____(1) Part A

_____(2) Part B

_____(3) Part D

_____(4) Part E

_____(5) Part F

3. What should Jan write in Part A?

_____(1)   the name of her bank

_____(2)   the date

_____(3)   her phone number

_____(4)   her Social Security number

_____(5)   nothing

4. Jan's ex-husband sends her child support payments. Where should she list this on the form?

_____(1)   Part A

_____(2)   Part B

_____(3)   Part C

_____(4)   Part D

_____(5)   nowhere

5. Jan has lived in her house for one year. What should she write in Part F?

_____(1)   her brother's address

_____(2)   her best friend's address

_____(3)   the address of the last place she lived

_____(4)   her ex-husband's new address

_____(5)   nothing

Answers start on page 94.

Review Exercise 5

George and Marie invited friends over to a cookout and party at a place called Clear Lake Villa. They gave directions so that no one would get lost. Their map is on the next page. Read through the 15 steps of the map. Picture yourself going through each one. Then answer the questions that follow.

HOW TO GET TO CLEAR LAKE VILLA

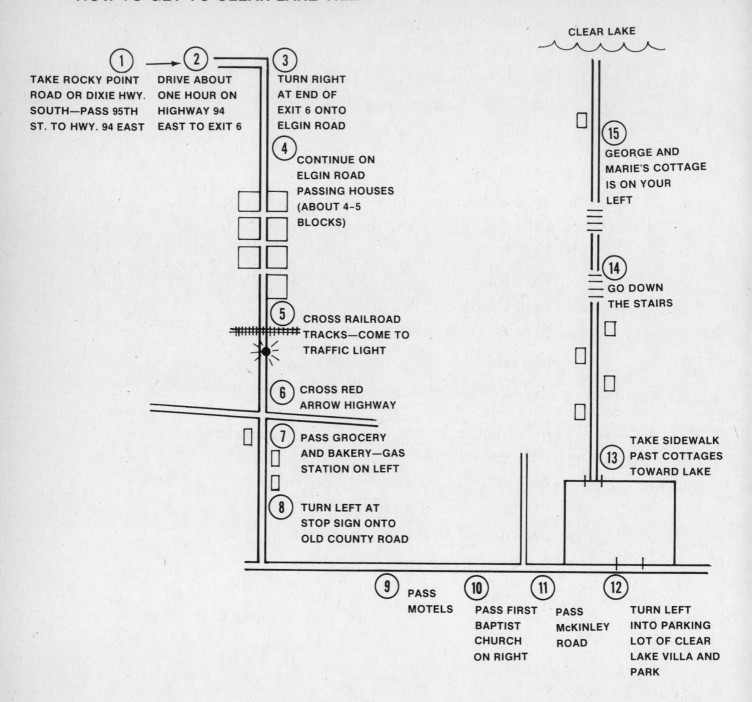

1. How will you travel based on what the directions say?

    _____ (1) You could go on foot.

    _____ (2) You would have to drive, then walk.

    _____ (3) You would walk first, then drive the last part only.

    _____ (4) You could drive the whole way.

_____(5) You would have to take a boat or a plane part of the way.

2. To get there by 2:00 p.m., what time should you start the trip?

_____(1) at 9:00 a.m.

_____(2) before 10:00 a.m.

_____(3) at noon

_____(4) before 1:00 p.m.

_____(5) by 1:30 p.m.

3. Which one of the following should NOT happen on the way to Clear Lake Villa

_____(1) You cross railroad tracks.

_____(2) At the Clear Lake Villa parking lot, you would turn left.

_____(3) At Old Country Road, you make a right turn.

_____(4) You pass McKinley Road.

_____(5) You drive along Elgin Road.

4. What do you do at Red Arrow Highway?

_____(1) cross it and keep going

_____(2) turn left

_____(3) turn right

_____(4) park and start walking

_____(5) go down the stairs

5. What exit do you take off Highway 94 East?

_____(1) No exit. The highway takes you right there.

_____(2) Exit 95

_____(3) Exit 1

_____(4) Exit 6

_____(5) the first exit after Elgin Road

ANSWERS AND EXPLANATIONS—PRACTICAL READING: FOLLOWING DIRECTIONS

Exercise 1

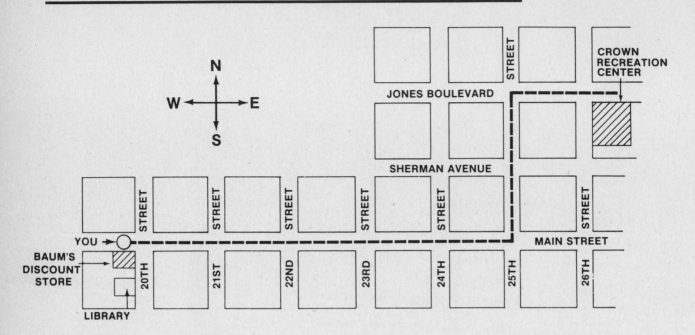

Exercise 2

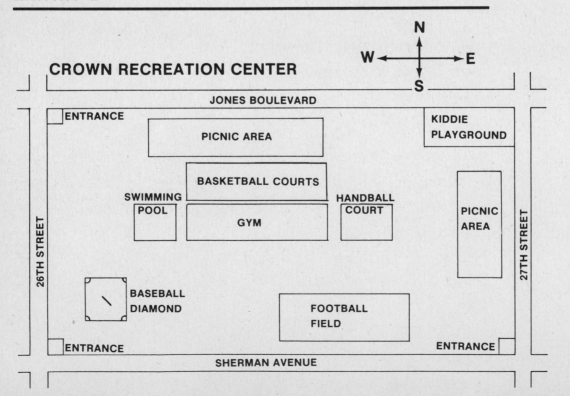

Exercise 3

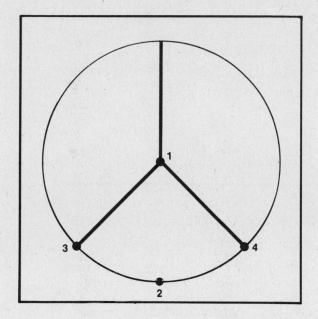

Exercise 4

1. (4) in a closed position with feet together
2. (2) She steps right when he steps left. The woman's part is the exact opposite of the man's part.
3. (1) slightly to the left in front of the right foot
4. (4) directly in front of the man's right foot
5. (5) step 7. Remember the woman does step 5, step 6 and step 7 when the man does step 2, step 3 and step 4.

Exercise 5

1. (2) Glue, string, pencil, cardboard. There is no need for string in this project. (1), (3), (4) and (5) list things used.
2. (4) is correct. Two hours includes time to let the glue dry.

3. (1) is the correct answer. This is found in the directions.

4. (5) None of the above will work. The directions call for a paperback book, not a hard-back book or a magazine.

5. (5) The directions call for white glue.

6. (2) None of the steps of the directions tells you to tie the paper to the book.

Exercise 6

1. (4) Seven; chocolate, sugar, corn syrup, light cream, salt, butter and vanilla extract.

2. (5) a candy thermometer; nowhere in the directions are we told to use this.

3. (5) when a drop of the chocolate forms a soft ball when it is dropped into cold water.

4. (2) butter; the recipe lists 2 tablespoons of butter along with the other ingredients. You also need a little more butter because the recipe says to lightly butter the inside of the pan.

5. (3) 1½ pounds; yield means how much the recipe will make.

6. Step 3: Bring to a boil over low heat and continue cooking—without stirring—until a drop of chocolate in cold water forms a soft ball—about 15 minutes.

Step 5: Let stand until lukewarm.

Step 7: Lightly butter inside of small square pan and add fudge.

Step 9: Cut into squares.

Exercise 7

1. (2) is correct. The directions say to do the exercise five times for each leg, for a total of ten times.
2. (4) It trims the waist. It also strengthens the stomach muscles.
3. (2) They should stay off the floor.
4. (3) is correct. The directions say that if you do the exercise each day, it is a good way to trim your waist and build strong stomach muscles.
5. (4) Straight out in front of you, off the floor.
6. Your steps might be written in other ways. This is a sample of how the steps might be written.
    1. Sit on the floor with your legs in front of you.
    2. Lean back resting on your hands.
    3. Bend your left knee and lift it up to your stomach.
    4. Pull your right leg straight, keeping it off the floor.
    5. Straighten one leg as you pull in the other.
You might also add:
    6. Repeat five times for each leg.
You could have broken your steps down differently.

Exercise 8

1. (3) Part C; Permanent Address
2. (1) Part A; Own Home, Rent, Board
3. (4) Part D; Ever Applied to This Company Before?
4. (5) Part E; Dependents Other Than Wife or Children
5. (2) Part B; If Related to Anyone in Our Employ, State Name and Department

Exercise 9

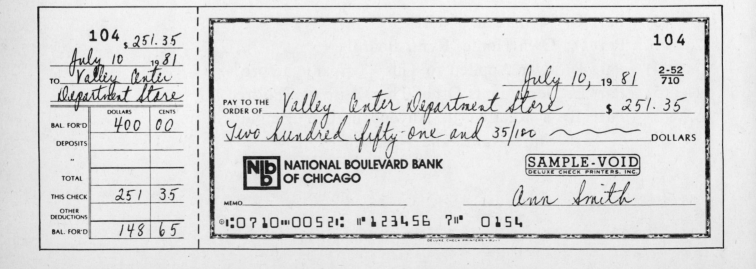

102 $34.02

July 10 1981

TO High Value Food Store

	DOLLARS	CENTS
BAL. FOR'D	100	00
DEPOSITS		
"		
TOTAL		
THIS CHECK	34	02
OTHER DEDUCTIONS		
BAL. FOR'D	65	98

102

PAY TO THE ORDER OF High Value Food Store   July 10, 1981   2-52/710 $ 34.02

Thirty-four and 02/100 ——————— DOLLARS

NATIONAL BOULEVARD BANK OF CHICAGO

SAMPLE-VOID   DELUXE CHECK PRINTERS, INC.

MEMO groceries   Ann Smith

⑆ 0710 0052 123456 7 0102

103 $132.00

July 10 1981

TO Gale's Fashion Clothes

	DOLLARS	CENTS
BAL. FOR'D	340	00
DEPOSITS		
"		
TOTAL		
THIS CHECK	132	00
OTHER DEDUCTIONS		
BAL. FOR'D	208	00

103

PAY TO THE ORDER OF Gale's Fashion Clothes   July 10, 1981   2-52/710 $ 132.00

One hundred thirty-two and 00/100 ——————— DOLLARS

NATIONAL BOULEVARD BANK OF CHICAGO

SAMPLE-VOID   DELUXE CHECK PRINTERS, INC.

MEMO winter coat   Ann Smith

⑆ 0710 0052 123456 7 0153

104 $251.35

July 10 1981

TO Valley Center Department Store

	DOLLARS	CENTS
BAL. FOR'D	400	00
DEPOSITS		
"		
TOTAL		
THIS CHECK	251	35
OTHER DEDUCTIONS		
BAL. FOR'D	148	65

104

PAY TO THE ORDER OF Valley Center Department Store   July 10, 1981   2-52/710 $ 251.35

Two hundred fifty-one and 35/100 ——————— DOLLARS

NATIONAL BOULEVARD BANK OF CHICAGO

SAMPLE-VOID   DELUXE CHECK PRINTERS, INC.

MEMO   Ann Smith

⑆ 0710 0052 123456 7 0154

ANSWERS AND EXPLANATIONS—REVIEW EXERCISES

Review Exercise 1

1. (3) crust, filling, topping
2. (2) ½ cup melted and ¼ cup soft
3. (3) 3 eggs; one to make the crust and topping and two to make the filling
4. (1) 15 people
5. (5) You bake it at 350° for 45-55 minutes.

Review Exercise 2

1. (2) four steps
2. (3) Jerk your wrist to make the yo-yo come back to your hand.
3. (3) Flick your wrist so the yo-yo goes inside your arm and down.
4. (4) Throwing the yo-yo out in front of you, slightly upward
5. (2) in your hand (hopefully)

Review Exercise 3

The H stands for home plate, the P for pitcher's box. The 1 is for first base, the 2 for second base, and the 3 for third. You should have drawn something that looks like a baseball diamond.

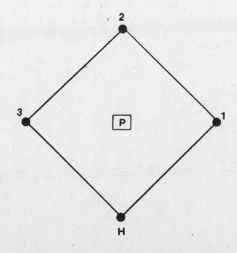

Review Exercise 4

1. (2) her brother's name
2. (3) Part D
3. (5) nothing
4. (2) Part B (But only if she wants this used as a basis for paying her charges.)
5. (3) the address of the last place she lived

Review Exercise 5

1. (2) You would have to drive, then walk.
2. (4) before 1:00 p.m. We know it will take at least one hour since Step 2 says to drive about one hour on Highway 94. The rest of the way should not take too much longer. Perhaps 10-15 minutes would get you from Exit 6 to the cottage.
3. (3) At Old Country Road, you make a right turn. See Step 8. You make a left turn.
4. (1) Cross it and keep going. See Step 6.
5. (4) Exit 6. See Step 2.

3 PRACTICAL READING: CHARTS AND ILLUSTRATIONS

Have you ever heard the saying, "A picture is worth a thousand words"? So far, all of the reading exercises in this book have been about reading words, paragraphs and passages. But there is another kind of reading. We read charts. We read diagrams. We read many other kinds of illustrations everyday. Often one picture or a good chart can show what it would take pages of writing to say.

Like following directions, reading charts and illustrations is something we do everyday. In fact, reading illustrations is often a part of following directions. If you are putting together shelves, a toy or a new gadget you have bought, the directions will often come with a diagram. Listings for trains, buses, planes and even television and radio shows are often given in the form of a chart or schedule. In this unit we will look at some of the different kinds of charts and illustrations you are likely to come across.

LOOKING AT DIAGRAMS

A **diagram** is one kind of illustration. It is often a line drawing that helps explain something. A diagram is just a picture. It can show where parts of something are found. It can show how to do something. It can show how to find a place. Diagrams are often found with parts labeled or with a special key to the symbols used. Diagrams are also used along with a set of directions or an explanation.

Exercise 1

The diagram shows some of the parts of the body that most suffer from bad habits like smoking cigarettes, not taking care of blood pressure, drinking too much alcohol and not watching your diet. Study the diagram. Then answer the questions that follow.

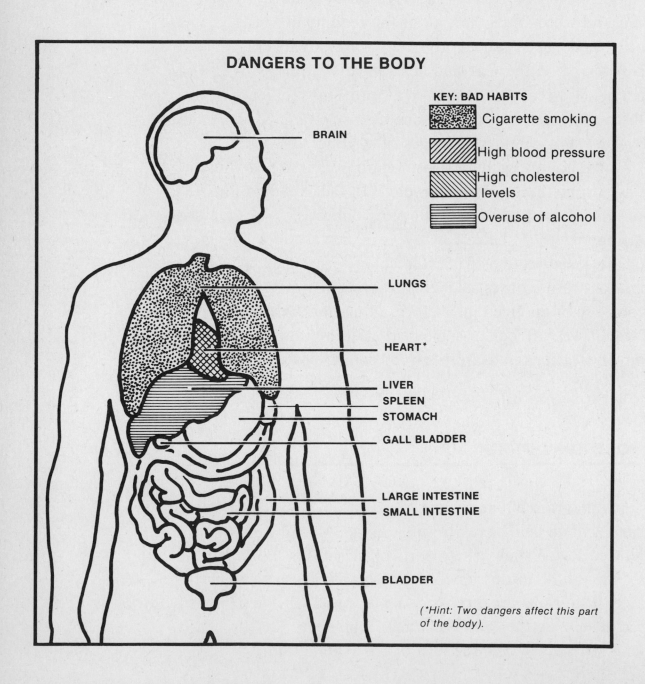

DANGERS TO THE BODY

KEY: BAD HABITS

Cigarette smoking

High blood pressure

High cholesterol levels

Overuse of alcohol

BRAIN

LUNGS

HEART*

LIVER

SPLEEN

STOMACH

GALL BLADDER

LARGE INTESTINE

SMALL INTESTINE

BLADDER

(*Hint: Two dangers affect this part of the body).

1. The diagram and key show that the bad habits listed harm the

   _____(1)   brain, lungs and bladder

   _____(2)   heart, lungs and liver

   _____(3)   liver, lungs and large intestine

   _____(4)   brain, stomach and liver

   _____(5)   stomach, small intestine and large intestine

2. The heart, according to the diagram, is most harmed by

   _____(1)   low blood pressure and low cholesterol

   _____(2)   high blood pressure and cigarette smoking

   _____(3)   low blood pressure and cigarette smoking

   _____(4)   overuse of alcohol and low blood pressure

   _____(5)   high blood pressure and high cholesterol

3. The diagram says that the part of the body that is harmed most by overuse of alcohol is

   _____(1)   the brain

   _____(2)   the liver

   _____(3)   the lungs

   _____(4)   the heart

   _____(5)   the bladder

4. What part of the body does cigarette smoking harm most, according to the diagram?

   _____(1)   the brain

   _____(2)   the liver

   _____(3)   the lungs

   _____(4)   the heart

   _____(5)   the bladder

5.   According to the information given, what parts of the body are NOT seriously harmed by these bad habits?

_____(1)   the spleen, stomach and lungs

_____(2)   the spleen, stomach and gall bladder

_____(3)   the lungs, stomach and heart

_____(4)   the spleen, stomach and liver

_____(5)   the heart, stomach and gall bladder

Answers start on page 133.

Exercise 2

Here is a short passage that shows a good way to use a fan to cool a house or apartment. There is a diagram with the passage. Read the passage and look at the diagram. Put a check mark (✔) in front of the best answer to the questions that follow.

Fan-Cooling Your Home

Air conditioners are one way to keep your home cool in the summer. But, because they cost a lot to buy and run, many people are using fans to keep their homes cool. You can cool a whole floor of your home with just one large fan if you put it in the right place.

There are two steps to fan-cooling your home. At night, use the fan to blow the warm air out of your house. Then, during the day, use it to keep cool air moving through the house.

The diagram shows exactly how to use the fan at night. Put the fan in front of a window so that it sucks the warm air out of your home. Close any other windows in that room. Open all doors between rooms. In the other rooms of the house, open all the windows. As the hot air is sucked out of the house, cool air will blow in through the open windows. This is a good way to keep your home cool all summer without spending a fortune.

How to cool two rooms at night with a fan.

1. The diagram and the passage are about

_____(1) using an air conditioner to cool your home.

_____(2) which windows to open during the day in winter.

_____(3) how to use a fan during hot weather to cool your home.

_____(4) cheap ways to clean your home.

_____(5) how to buy the best fan to cool your house.

2. What do the arrows in the diagram stand for?

_____(1) how a fan blows air out of a house during the day

_____(2) how heat moves in and out of a house at night

_____(3) how cool air can move from a window through the rooms at night

_____(4) moving cool air around a house during the day

_____(5) none of the above

3. At night you put a fan by an open window in one room. What should you do about the other windows in this room?

_____(1)   Open all of them.

_____(2)   Open them all halfway.

_____(3)   Keep one open and one shut.

_____(4)   Close all of them.

_____(5)   The diagram does not give this information.

4. According to the passage and diagram, where should the fan be placed at night.

_____(1)   facing the room with the door opened

_____(2)   in the middle of the bedroom

_____(3)   in the living room window

_____(4)   facing an open bedroom window

_____(5)   The diagram does not show this.

5. During the day, you close all the windows and use the fan to keep the cool air moving. At night, you use the fan to

_____(1)   blow the cool air out of your house.

_____(2)   keep the warm air moving upward.

_____(3)   blow the warm air out of your house.

_____(4)   keep your electricity going.

_____(5)   pull in warm air.

Answers start on page 133.

READING CHARTS

Reading a chart is another way to get information. A **chart** is like a diagram. Charts can be made up of rows and columns of information, news or facts. Often a chart will use signs or symbols. There should always be a **key** at the top or bottom of the chart to tell you what the symbols mean.

Exercise 3

Study this chart. Answer the questions that follow. Put a check mark (✓) in front of the best answer.

FISHING FORECAST AT LAKE KENNY			
WYOMING		Wheatland	Some fishermen have been getting rainbows and brown trout.
		Hannah	Trout, mornings and late afternoons below the dam.
UTAH		Rainbow Bridge	Steelhead and trout around mouth of Trail Creek. Excellent fishing.
COLORADO		Two Rivers	Steelhead at the creek mouth, caught on worms.
		Durango	Steelhead, occasional brown trout—very spotty fishing.
ARIZONA		Glen Canyon	Steelhead and brown trout from piers. Cold.
		Flagstaff	Some steelhead at mouth of St. Joe River.

KEY: excellent
        good
        fair

1. This is a chart that shows
    _____(1)   fishing areas in the United States.
    _____(2)   how the fish are biting at different spots on Lake Kenny.
    _____(3)   the best places to fish in Washington and Oregon.

_____(4) how the fishing is in Colorado and Wisconsin rivers.

_____(5) the best kinds of fish.

2. This means

_____(1) no fishing.

_____(2) good fishing.

_____(3) excellent fishing.

_____(4) fair fishing.

_____(5) none of the above

3. An excellent place to find steelhead and trout is

_____(1) Rainbow Bridge.

_____(2) Two Rivers.

_____(3) Flagstaff.

_____(4) Durango.

_____(5) Glen Canyon.

4. Steelhead and brown trout are very spotty at

_____(1) Two Rivers

_____(2) Wheatland.

_____(3) Hannah.

_____(4) Glen Canyon.

_____(5) Durango.

5. An excellent place to find trout in the mornings and late afternoons is

_____(1) the creek mouth at Two Rivers, Colorado.

_____(2) Durango, Colorado.

_____(3) Wheatland, Wyoming.

_____(4) at Hannah, Wyoming, below the dam.

_____(5) in Flagstaff, at the mouth of the St. Joe River.

Answers start on page 133.

Exercise 4

Fans' Poll

Students at Miller's High School voted for their favorite college basketball teams. Here are the results:

(First-place votes in parentheses)

	Team	W	L	Pts.
1.	DePaul (274)	6	0	3,903
2.	Kentucky (78)	4	0	3,595
3.	UCLA (11)	5	0	2,989
4.	Virginia (1)	5	0	2,010
5.	Illinois (31)	4	0	1,553
6.	Indiana (4)	5	2	1,467
7.	Oregon State (4)	5	0	1,284
8.	Maryland	5	1	1,218
9.	Notre Dame	4	1	1,088
10.	North Carolina	6	1	984
11.	Ohio State	2	2	969
12.	Michigan (1)	6	0	514
13.	Louisville	1	3	462
14.	Iowa (4)	5	1	392
15.	Purdue (1)	5	1	294
16.	Louisiana State (3)	4	1	157
17.	Marquette (1)	4	1	146
18.	Bradley (3)	4	1	117
19.	Texas A&M	5	0	116
20.	Missouri	6	2	101

Key: W: wins so far this season
L: losses so far this season
Pts.: total points gained in games this season

1. This chart is about
    _____(1)   winning basketball teams at Miller High School.
    _____(2)   a poll of Miller's High School students' favorite college basketball teams.
    _____(3)   the top 20 basketball teams in the U.S.
    _____(4)   the winning and losing scores of 20 basketball teams.
    _____(5)   none of the above

2. Which team won first-place in the fans' poll?
    _____(1)   UCLA
    _____(2)   Iowa
    _____(3)   DePaul
    _____(4)   Texas
    _____(5)   Bradley

3. What does "W" stand for?
    _____(1)   withdrawn for the season
    _____(2)   without any penalties for the season
    _____(3)   winnings from last year
    _____(4)   wins so far this season
    _____(5)   The chart does not give this information.

4. How many losses has Texas A&M had this season?
    _____(1)   0
    _____(2)   1

_____(3) 3
_____(4) 2
_____(5) 4

5. How many teams did not get any first place votes?
_____(1) 5
_____(2) 0
_____(3) 1
_____(4) 8
_____(5) 7

Answers start on page 134.

UNDERSTANDING LISTINGS AND SCHEDULES

A listing of the times that things happen is called a **schedule.** Schedules are another handy way to gather information. They can tell you what train or bus to catch, what's playing on TV or at the movies or what is planned for a certain day, week or month. There are many kinds of schedules.

Exercise 5

Study this train schedule. Look at the key. Then answer the questions that follow. Make a check mark (✔) by the best choice.

Pacific Central Train Schedule
Clarksville—Monroe

Read down		Gate 5	Gate 7	Gate 8
		♪ ♫		
		RR	M.T.	☎
		M-S	M-S	H
Leave	Clarksville	6:15 A.M.	7:10 A.M.	12:15 P.M.
Leave	Lunt	6:30 A.M.	—	12:30 P.M.
	Round Lake	—	—	—
	Brownsville	—	—	—
Leave	Kramer	—	7:55 A.M.	12:45 P.M.
	Cedar Lake	7:00 A.M.	—	—
	London	—	—	—
	Blufford	—		—
Leave	Rand Forest	—	8:15 A.M.	—
	Deer Park	7:20 A.M.	8:25 A.M.	1:30 P.M.
	Clearbrook	7:30 A.M.	—	—
Leave	Melton Park	—	—	—
	Greenwood	—	—	2:00 P.M.
	Bryn Mawr	—	9:00 A.M.	—
Leave	Elk City	—	—	2:30 P.M.
	Leeds	—	9:30 A.M.	—
	Monroe	8:00 A.M.	9:40 A.M.	2:45 P.M.

Key

H	Train stops to pick up passengers on Sundays and holidays only.
M-S	Train stops to pick up passengers Monday through Saturday except holidays.
M.T.	Mail train
♪ ♫	Music
☎	Telephones
RR	Restrooms on board

1. This schedule shows trains from
    _____(1)   Gate 8, Monday through Saturday.
    _____(2)   Gate 5, Holidays and Sundays.
    _____(3)   Clarksville to Monroe.
    _____(4)   Lunt to Rand Forest only.
    _____(5)   Clarksville to Lunt only.

2. On Christmas Day, what time could you catch a train
    from Kramer to Monroe?
    _____(1)   7:55 A.M.
    _____(2)   12:45 P.M.
    _____(3)   12:15 P.M.
    _____(4)   2:45 P.M.
    _____(5)   There would be no train that day.

3. On Christmas Day, to take the train from Kramer to
    Monroe, where should you go?
    _____(1)   Gate 5
    _____(2)   Gate 7
    _____(3)   Gate 8
    _____(4)   Gate 5, 7 or 8
    _____(5)   There would be no train that day.

4. On a Monday, what would be the earliest train leaving
    Clarksville?
    _____(1)   7:10 A.M.
    _____(2)   12:15 P.M.
    _____(3)   5:00 A.M.
    _____(4)   1:30 P.M.
    _____(5)   6:15 A.M.

5. To go from Deer Park to Elk City you should
    _____(1)   Catch the 7:20 A.M. train at Gate 5.
    _____(2)   Catch the 1:30 P.M. train at Gate 8.

_____(3)   Catch the 8:25 A.M. train at Gate 7.

_____(4)   (1), (2) or (3).

_____(5)   (1) or (2) only.

Answers start on page 134.

Exercise 6

Look at this TV schedule. Study the key. Answer the questions that follow.

Friday

========================

EVENING

6:00

2 CBS MOVIE * LOVE ME OR LEAVE ME (1955)

5 ROCKFORD FILES (R)

7 ABC MOVIE ** AMERICAN GIGOLO (1979)

11 CHICAGO WEEK IN REVIEW

26 POLKA PARTY

32 DINAH! & FRIENDS

44 700 CLUB

6:30

11 NOVA (C)

38 TIMELINE

7:00

5 FAMILY FEUD (R)

11 THE NAKED CIVIL SERVANT

32 ROOKIES (R)

38 GOOD NEWS

7:30

38 JIMMY SWAGGART

44 STAR TREK (R)

7:55

32 NEWS

8:00

9 WALL STREET JOURNAL BUSINESS REPORT (C)

8:30

2 5 7 9 NEWS (C)

26 INFORMACION 26 (SPANISH NEWS)

32 BRADY BUNCH (R)

44 DRAGNET (R)

9:00

2 LOU GRANT

5 QUINCY

7 CHARLIE'S ANGELS

9 MOVIE *** THE BLOODY VAMPIRE (1963)

11 MOVIE *** BIRTH OF THE BLUES (1941)

26 THIS OLD HOUSE

32 PARTRIDGE FAMILY

38 PTL CLUB

44 MOVIE * THE COUNT OF MONTE CRISTO (1934)

32 MAKE ME LAUGH

9:55

26 MOVIE ** VIOLENT SATURDAY

32 NEWSTALK

10:00

7 FRIDAY NIGHT MOVIE ** THE HUNTERS (1974)

2 CBS LATE MOVIE ** MALAYA (1950)

5 MIDNIGHT SPECIAL

32 JUKEBOX

KEY

(R) repeat	* Time-Waster
(C) captions for the hearing-impaired	** OK
	*** Excellent

1. This schedule shows
   _____(1) holiday TV listings.
   _____(2) radio listings.
   _____(3) movie listings only.
   _____(4) all comedy shows.
   _____(5) Friday night TV listings.

2. Which of these shows can be seen at 9:00 p.m.?
   _____(1) Star Trek
   _____(2) Good News
   _____(3) Charlie's Angels
   _____(4) Friday Night Movie
   _____(5) Spanish News

3. What time does the first movie start on Friday evening?
   _____(1) 9:00 P.M.
   _____(2) 6:00 P.M.
   _____(3) 6:30 P.M.
   _____(4) 10:00 P.M.
   _____(5) 7:00 P.M.

4. What is the last movie shown on Friday evening?
   _____(1) Make Me Laugh
   _____(2) Birth of the Blues
   _____(3) Friday Night Movie—The Hunters (1974)
   _____(4) CBS Movie—Love Me or Leave Me (1955)
   _____(5) The Count of Monte Cristo

5. What channel and time is Nova on?

_____(1)   Channel 11 at 9:00 P.M.

_____(2)   Channel 11 at 7:00 P.M.

_____(3)   Channel 11 at 6:30 P.M.

_____(4)   Channel 38 at 6:30 P.M.

_____(5)   Channel 5 at 10:00 P.M.

6. What could you watch at 7:55 P.M.?

_____(1)   News

_____(2)   CBS Movie

_____(3)   Juke Box

_____(4)   Dragnet

_____(5)   PTL Club

7. Which channels show the news at 8:30?

_____(1)   2, 5 and 7 only

_____(2)   2, 5, 7, 9 and 26

_____(3)   32

_____(4)   44

_____(5)   All the channels

8. Which is the best of the movies listed below based on this TV schedule?

_____(1)   Violent Saturday, 9:55 P.M.

_____(2)   Love Me or Leave Me, 6:00 P.M.

_____(3)   Birth of the Blues, 9:00 P.M.

_____(4)   The Hunters, 10:00 P.M.

_____(5)   Malaya, 10:00 P.M.

9. Which of the following shows is NOT a repeat?

_____(1)   Midnight Special at 10:00 P.M.

_____(2)   Brady Bunch at 8:30 P.M.

_____(3)   Star Trek at 7:30 P.M.

_____(4)   Rookies at 7:00 P.M.

_____(5)   Family Feud at 7:00 P.M.

10.   Which is the worst of the movies listed below based on this TV schedule?

_____(1)   The Bloody Vampire, 9:00 P.M.

_____(2)   American Gigolo, 6:00 P.M.

_____(3)   Malaya, 10:00 P.M.

_____(4)   The Count of Monte Cristo, 9:00 P.M.

_____(5)   The Hunters, 10:00 P.M.

Answers start on page 134.

LOOKING AT GRAPHS

A **graph** is like both diagrams and charts. Graphs can give lots of information and can show relationships. They can quickly help you compare different numbers or amounts. Here, we will work with three kinds of graphs: circle graphs, line graphs and bar graphs.

Understanding Circle Graphs

One simple type of graph is called a circle or pie graph. The circle shows the total amount of something. It might show the total number of children in a city or the total number of hot dogs eaten in New York in 1967 or the total number of hours in a day. The circle is divided into wedges. These pie slices stand for different parts of the whole. Here is an example of a pie graph:

WHO GROWS COTTON—1980 WORLD PRODUCTION—58.6 MILLION BALES

The circle in this graph stands for the total amount of cotton grown in the world in 1980. The wedges show how much of that total each of the listed countries grows. By looking at the graph can you tell which country is the largest grower of cotton in the world? Which country is second in the amount of cotton it grows? Write your answers here:

Largest cotton producer: _____

Second largest: _____

You read the graph correctly if you wrote that the U.S. is the world's largest producer of cotton. The second largest single producer of cotton is the U.S.S.R. You can see on the graph that "Other" has the second biggest wedge. "Other" means all the countries in the world that are not listed. All of these countries grow amounts of cotton smaller than the 4% listed for Egypt. All of these countries together grow 20% of the world's cotton.

Exercise 7

Study this pie graph. Answer the questions that follow it by putting a check mark (✔) in front of the best answer.

HOW FAMILY INCOME IS SPENT IN A YEAR

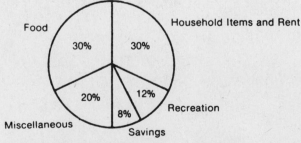

Total Family Income = $12,000

1. What portion of this family's budget is spent on food?

_____(1)   20%

_____(2)   60%

_____(3)   30%

_____(4)   12%

_____(5)   8%

2. What part of its income does the family spend on recreation each year?

_____(1)   20%

_____(2)   8%

_____(3)   30%

_____(4)   12%

_____(5)   It is impossible to tell from the graph.

3. Which one of the items listed on the graph uses up the largest part of the family income?

_____(1)   miscellaneous expenses

_____(2)   recreation

_____(3)   The family saves most of its money.

_____(4)   Food and household items and rent are the biggest slices and take the same amount of income.

_____(5)   Household items and rent are the biggest expense.

4. Which of the items shown on the graph takes up the least income?

_____(1)   food

_____(2)   savings

_____(3)   recreation

_____(4)   clothing

_____(5)   buying Christmas presents

5. What is the total family income?

_____(1)   You can't tell by the graph.

_____(2) $30,000

_____(3) $20,000

_____(4) $8,000

_____(5) $12,000

Answers start on page 135.

Understanding Bar Graphs

A bar graph shows different amounts by using bars or strips of different lengths. A bar graph might show the number of high school graduates in the United States in 1980 as compared to the number in 1975. A bar graph could show the number of babies born or the number of working women each year. In a bar graph each bar is labeled to show what it stands for.

Exercise 8

Study the bar graph that follows. Check the best answer to each question.

PARTICIPANTS IN FAVORITE AMERICAN PASTIMES

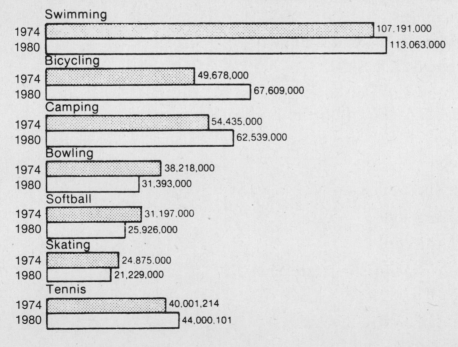

Swimming
1974 107,191,000
1980 113,063,000

Bicycling
1974 49,678,000
1980 67,609,000

Camping
1974 54,435,000
1980 62,539,000

Bowling
1974 38,218,000
1980 31,393,000

Softball
1974 31,197,000
1980 25,926,000

Skating
1974 24,875,000
1980 21,229,000

Tennis
1974 40,001,214
1980 44,000,101

1. What seems to be the favorite American pastime?
   _____(1) tennis
   _____(2) jogging
   _____(3) bicycling
   _____(4) swimming
   _____(5) reading

2. How many pastimes attracted more people in 1980 than in 1974?
   _____(1) all of them
   _____(2) none of them
   _____(3) four: tennis, camping, bicycling and swimming
   _____(4) three: swimming, camping and tennis
   _____(5) two: bicycling and bowling

3. Which pastimes attracted fewer people in 1980 than in 1974?
   _____(1) swimming and camping
   _____(2) bowling, softball and skating
   _____(3) softball and skating
   _____(4) tennis and skating
   _____(5) tennis and bowling

4. How many people went camping in 1974?
   _____(1) 54,435,000
   _____(2) 62,539,000
   _____(3) 49,678,000
   _____(4) 38,218,000
   _____(5) 31,197,000

5. Which pastime grew the most between 1974 and 1980?

_____(1) swimming

_____(2) camping

_____(3) tennis

_____(4) bicycling

_____(5) Bicycling and camping gained the same number.

Answers start on page 135.

Looking at Line Graphs

A line graph shows a changing relationship between things.

GROWTH IN AUTO REGISTRATION

This line graph shows the number of cars registered each year from 1920 through 1965. Along the bottom of the graph, the years are listed. The number of cars registered is listed along the left side of the graph. It is very common for the bottom of a line graph to list some unit of time. In this case the unit is years. (In other cases the unit will be months or days or hours.)

Whenever a time unit is listed on the bottom of a line graph, the graph will show how something has changed through time. In this case the graph will show how the number of cars registered has changed through time.

To read this line graph look at the bottom where the years are given. Then look at the left-hand side of the graph. The left-hand side tells you the number of motor vehicles registered. You can tell how many vehicles were registered in a given year by following the heavy jagged line and seeing where it meets the vertical lines of the graph.

For instance, in 1925, 20 million cars were registered. By 1930 the number had gone up to about 30 million. There isn't a line running across the graph for 30 million, so for 1930, you will have to guess the number of cars. In 1955, 60 million cars were registered.

Exercise 9

Here are some more questions for you to answer about this line graph.

1. About how many autos were registered in 1960?
   _____(1) about 60 million
   _____(2) about 65 million
   _____(3) about 70 million
   _____(4) about 75 million
   _____(5) about 80 million

2. Over which five-year periods were there no increases in the number of cars registered?
   _____(1) 1930-1935, 1940-1945
   _____(2) 1950-1955, 1930-1935
   _____(3) 1940-1945, 1960-1965
   _____(4) 1915-1920, 1930-1935
   _____(5) 1945-1950, 1955-1960

3. Overall, what has happened to the number of cars registered since 1920?

_____(1)   There was a decrease until 1950, when there was a sharp increase.

_____(2)   First there was an increase, then a sharp decrease.

_____(3)   The number has stayed about the same.

_____(4)   Overall the number has decreased.

_____(5)   Overall the number has increased.

4. About how many cars were registered in 1955?

_____(1)   60 million

_____(2)   70 million

_____(3)   80 million

_____(4)   90 million

_____(5)   100 million

5. How many cars were registered in 1965?

_____(1)   60 million

_____(2)   70 million

_____(3)   80 million

_____(4)   90 million

_____(5)   100 million

Answers start on page 135.

Exercise 10

This is a graph of the population changes in three cities. Study the graph. Answer the questions that follow by marking a check mark (✔) by the best choice.

POPULATION GROWTH FOR THREE CITIES

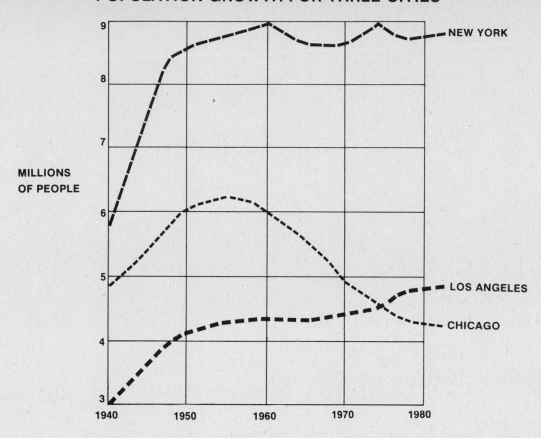

1. This graph looks at population changes between

_____(1)   1940 and 1950.

_____(2)   1970 and 1980.

_____(3)   1940 and 1980.

_____(4)   1950 and 1960.

_____(5)   1960 and 1980.

2. In 1960, Chicago had

_____(1)   more people than Los Angeles.

_____(2)   fewer people than Los Angeles.

_____(3)   more people than New York.

_____(4)   about the same number of people as New York.

_____(5)   about the same number of people as Los Angeles.

3. In 1980, Chicago had

    _____(1)   more people than Los Angeles.

    _____(2)   fewer people than Los Angeles.

    _____(3)   more people than New York.

    _____(4)   about the same number of people as New
                  York

    _____(5)   about the same number of people as Los
                  Angeles.

4. When did New York have its greatest number of
    people?

    _____(1)   in 1980

    _____(2)   in 1960

    _____(3)   in 1965 and about 1973

    _____(4)   in 1960 and about 1973

    _____(5)   in 1960 and 1980

5. When did Chicago have its greatest number of people?

    _____(1)   1970-1980

    _____(2)   1960-1970

    _____(3)   1950-1960

    _____(4)   1940-1950

    _____(5)   1930-1940

Answers start on page 135.

REVIEW EXERCISES—PRACTICAL READING: ILLUSTRATIONS

Review Exercise 1

Here is a pie graph which shows the sources of income for public colleges in the U.S. The circle stands for each dollar of income for the colleges. Use the graph to answer the questions that follow.

SOURCES OF INCOME—PUBLIC COLLEGES OF U.S.

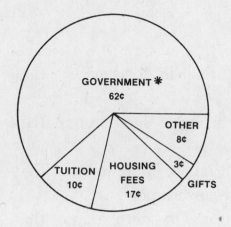

* Government refers to all levels of government—not exclusively the federal government.

1. What is the biggest source of income for the public colleges?
    _____(1)   tuition
    _____(2)   government
    _____(3)   housing fees
    _____(4)   gifts
    _____(5)   other

2. Housing fees bring the colleges how many cents of each dollar of income?
    _____(1)   10¢
    _____(2)   17¢
    _____(3)   62¢
    _____(4)   7¢
    _____(5)   3¢

3. Which source brings in the least amount of income?

_____(1) tuition

_____(2) housing fees

_____(3) gifts

_____(4) government

_____(5) benefits

4. Which of these is true?

_____(1) Housing fees bring in less money than gifts.

_____(2) Housing fees bring in less money than tuition.

_____(3) Housing fees bring in more money than comes from the government.

_____(4) Housing fees bring in more money than tuition.

_____(5) Housing fees bring in as much money as tuition does.

5. Which of these is true?

_____(1) Tuition brings in more money than gifts.

_____(2) Tuition brings in less money than gifts.

_____(3) Tuition brings in more money than housing fees.

_____(4) Tuition brings in as much money as housing fees.

_____(5) Tuition brings in as much money as other sources.

Answers start on page 136.

Review Exercise 2

Here is a line graph that gives information on salaries for teachers who have master's degrees. The graph relates years of teaching experience to salary. Use the graph to answer the questions that follow.

TEACHER SALARY—MASTER'S DEGREE SCALE

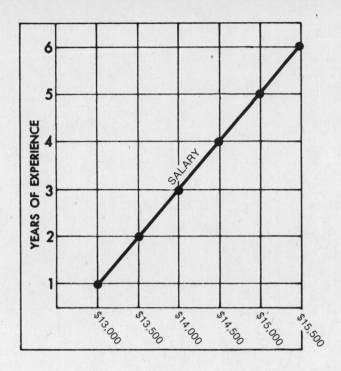

1. This graph shows
    _____(1)   years needed to earn a master's degree.
    _____(2)   teachers' salaries with master's degrees.
    _____(3)   teachers' salaries in 1970-1980.
    _____(4)   teachers' salaries in public schools.
    _____(5)   teachers' salaries in private schools with
                master's degrees.

2. A teacher with two years of experience and a master's
    degree will earn
    _____(1) $13,000.
    _____(2) $13,500.
    _____(3) $14,000.
    _____(4) $14,500.
    _____(5) $15,000.

3. A teacher with five years of experience and a master's degree will earn

_____(1) $13,000.

_____(2) $13,500.

_____(3) $14,000.

_____(4) $14,500.

_____(5) $15,000.

4. If a teacher with a master's degree is making $14,500 how long has he or she been teaching?

_____(1)   one year

_____(2)   two years

_____(3)   three years

_____(4)   four years

_____(5)   five years

5. After eight years of experience, what do you think the salary would be for a teacher with a master's degree?

_____(1) $15,500

_____(2) $16,000

_____(3) $16,500

_____(4) $17,000

_____(5) $17,500

Answers start on page 136.

Review Exercise 3

Study this train schedule. Then answer the questions that follow.

NORTHBOUND

MONDAYS THROUGH SATURDAYS EXCEPT HOLIDAYS AND WHERE OTHERWISE INDICATED

Train No.	Leave 10th St.	Leave 9th St.	Leave 8th St.	Leave 7th St.	Leave 5th St.	Leave 3rd St.	Leave 1st St.	Arrive Madison
	A.M.	A.M.	A.M.	A.M.	A.M.	A.M.	A.M.	A.M.
M-S104	6:10	6:11	6:13	f 6:14	f 6:17	6:19	f 6:20	6:28
M-S306	6:54	6:56	6:58	......	7:02	7:04	......	7:13
M-F500	7:04	7:06	7:08	......	......	......	......	7:22
M-F750	7:06	......	......	......	......	......	......	7:23
M-F400	7:18	7:20	7:22	......	7:26	7:28	......	7:37
M-F502	......	7:24	......	......	......	......	......	7:40
M-F732	......	7:26	......	......	......	......	......	7:41
M-F702	......	7:29	......	......	......	......	......	7:44
S-108	7:32	......	......	......	......	7:38	......	7:48
M-F110	7:29	7:31	7:33	7:34	7:37	7:39	7:40	7:48
S-308	7:37	7:38	7:40	f 7:41	f 7:44	7:46	f 7:47	7:55
M-F402	7:38	7:40	7:42	......	7:46	7:48	......	7:57
M-F604	7:51	7:53	7:55	7:56	7:59	8:01	......	8:10
S-212	8:00	......	......	......	......	......	......	8:14
S-112	8:02	......	......	......	......	......	......	8:16
M-F408	7:58	8:00	8:02	......	8:06	8:08	......	8:17
M-F758	8:07	......	8:10	......	......	......	......	8:23
S-312	8:07	8:08	8:10	f 8:11	f 8:14	8:16	f 8:17	8:25
M-F506	8:08	8:10	8:12	8:13	8:16	8:18	8:19	8:27
M-F708	8:15	......	8:18	......	......	......	......	8:32
M-F410	8:18	8:20	8:22	......	8:26	8:28	......	8:37
M-F760	8:26	......	......	......	......	......	......	8:41
S-116	......	......	......	......	......	......	......	8:46
M-F710	8:32	......	......	......	......	......	......	8:47
M-F508	8:34	8:35	8:37	......	......	......	......	8:50
M-F412	8:38	8:40	8:42	......	8:46	8:48	......	8:57
M-S218	9:00	......	......	......	......	......	......	9:14
M-S118	9:02	......	......	......	......	......	......	9:16
M-S318	9:07	9:08	9:10	f 9:11	f 9:14	9:16	f, 9:17	9:25
M-S120	9:32	......	......	......	......	......	......	9:46
M-S320	9:37	9:38	9:40	f 9:41	f 9:44	9:46	f 9:47	9:55
M-S222	10:00	7:29	......	......	......	......	......	10:14
M-S322	10:07	10:08	10:10	f 10:11	f 10:14	10:16	f 10:17	10:25
M-S124	10:32	......	......	......	......	......	......	10:46
M-S324	10:37	10:38	10:40	f 10:41	f 10:44	10:46	f 10:47	10:55
	A.M.	A.M.	A.M.	A.M.	A.M.	A.M.	A.M.	A.M.

Key
M-S: Monday through Saturday
M-F: Monday through Friday
S: Saturdays only
f: Flag Stop Notify Trainman

1. This schedule shows

_____(1)   trains from 1st to 10th on holidays.

_____(2)   trains from 9th to Madison Mondays through Fridays.

_____(3)   trains northbound from 10th to 21st Street.

_____(4)   trains northbound from 10th to Madison.

_____(5)   trains from 23rd to 10th Street.

2. To arrive at Madison at 9:25 A.M. what train should you take?

_____(1)   M-S218

_____(2)   M-S118

_____(3)   M-S318

_____(4)   M-S120

_____(5)   M-S320

3. How many stops does that train make between 10th Street and Madison?

_____(1)   eight stops including 10th Street and Madison

_____(2)   seven stops including 10th Street and Madison

_____(3)   six stops including 10th Street and Madison

_____(4)   five stops including 10th Street and Madison

_____(5)   four stops including 10th Street and Madison

4. To get off the train at 7th Street at 9:11 A.M., what must you do?

_____(1)   nothing

_____(2)   Notify the trainman.

_____(3)   Push a button.

_____(4)   There is no stop at 7th Street at 9:11 A.M.

_____(5)   Be careful to stay out of sight.

5. Which of the following trains could you take on a Saturday to go from 9th Street to Madison and arrive before 8:00 A.M.?

_____(1)   M-F702

_____(2)   S-112

_____(3)   S-108

_____(4)   M-F110

_____(5)   S-308

Answers start on page 136.

Review Exercise 4

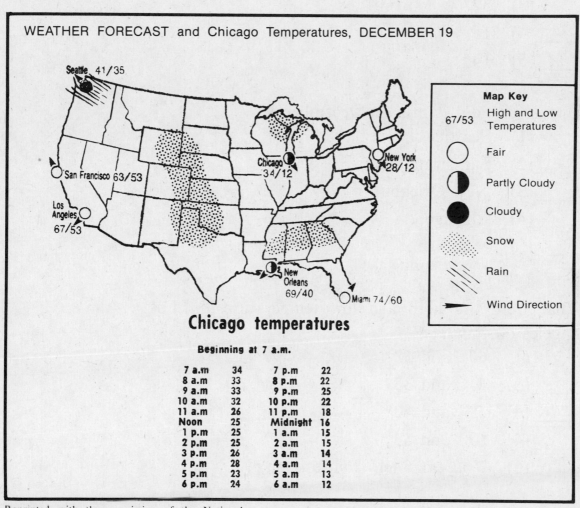

WEATHER FORECAST and Chicago Temperatures, DECEMBER 19

Seattle 41/35

San Francisco 63/53

Los Angeles 67/53

Chicago 34/12

New York 28/12

New Orleans 69/40

Miami 74/60

Map Key

| 67/53 | High and Low Temperatures |
| Fair |
| Partly Cloudy |
| Cloudy |
| Snow |
| Rain |
| Wind Direction |

Chicago temperatures

Beginning at 7 a.m.

7 a.m	34	7 p.m	22
8 a.m	33	8 p.m	22
9 a.m	33	9 p.m	25
10 a.m	32	10 p.m	22
11 a.m	26	11 p.m	18
Noon	25	Midnight	16
1 p.m	25	1 a.m	15
2 p.m	25	2 a.m	15
3 p.m	26	3 a.m	14
4 p.m	28	4 a.m	14
5 p.m	23	5 a.m	13
6 p.m	24	6 a.m	12

Reprinted with the permission of the National Oceanic and Atmospheric Administration.

1. This map and chart show

_____(1)   high and low pressure areas.

_____(2)   temperatures for all U.S. cities.

_____(3)   weather in the U.S. and Chicago temperatures.

_____(4) wind directions and pressure areas.

_____(5) where it is snowing and raining in the U.S.

2. At 1 P.M. on Thursday, what was the temperature in Chicago?

_____(1) 34°

_____(2) 25°

_____(3) 32°

_____(4) 15°

_____(5) 14°

3. In what city did it rain on December 19?

_____(1) Seattle

_____(2) San Francisco

_____(3) New Orleans

_____(4) Chicago

_____(5) Miami

4. What were the high and low temperatures in Los Angeles on this day?

_____(1) 63° and 53°

_____(2) 41° and 35°

_____(3) 59° and 40°

_____(4) 67° and 53°

_____(5) You can't tell from this map.

5. In which cities was it partly cloudy on this day?

_____(1) Chicago and New Orleans

_____(2) Chicago and New York

_____(3) New York and Miami

_____(4) Miami and New Orleans

_____(5) San Francisco and Chicago

Answers start on page 136.

Review Exercise 5

A solar system is made up of a star and the planets that move around the star. Our sun is a star, just like the stars you see in the sky at night. Our sun seems so large and bright because it is so much closer to us than the other stars. The planets in our solar system are Mercury, Venus, Earth, Mars, Jupiter, Saturn, Uranus, Neptune and Pluto. The diagram that follows shows the order of the different planets in our solar system.

THE SOLAR SYSTEM

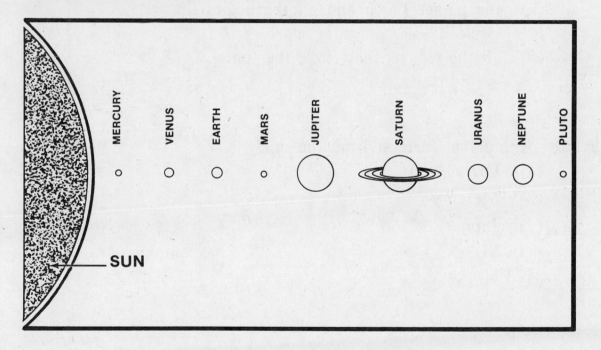

1. This is a diagram of
   _____(1)   the planets that orbit the sun.
   _____(2)   the stars that orbit the sun.
   _____(3)   the planet Earth.
   _____(4)   the moon.
   _____(5)   the planet Jupiter.

2. How many planets are there in our solar system?

_____(1)   seven

_____(2)   eight

_____(3)   nine

_____(4)   four

_____(5)   five

3. What is the solar system made up of?

_____(1)   the sun and all bodies that circle it

_____(2)   the sun, Earth and stars

_____(3)   the sun, moon and stars

_____(4)   the planet Earth and all the bodies that circle it

_____(5)   all the planets that circle the sun.

4. What is the planet furthest from the sun?

_____(1)   Earth

_____(2)   Mercury

_____(3)   Jupiter

_____(4)   Mars

_____(5)   Pluto

5. Which planet is between Jupiter and Uranus?

_____(1)   Neptune

_____(2)   Pluto

_____(3)   Earth

_____(4)   Saturn

_____(5)   Mars

Answers start on page 137.

Review Exercise 6

Study this chart. Then answer the questions that follow.

Ten most fuel-efficient cars
All manual transmissions
In miles per gallon

Volkswagen Rabbit diesel (4-speed)	42
Toyota Starlet (5-speed)	39
Volkswagen Rabbit diesel (5-speed)	38
Dodge Colt (4-speed)	37
Plymouth Champ (4-speed)	37
Datsun 210 (5-speed)	36
Toyota Corolla Tercel (4-speed)	36
Honda Civic (5-speed)	35
Mazda GLC (4-speed)	35
Mazda GLC (5-speed)	35

3 top American cars

Chevrolet Chevette (4-speed)	30
Ford Escort (4-speed)	30
Lincoln-Mercury Lynx (4-speed)	30

Source: Environmental Protection Agency

Chicago Tribune Graphic

1. Which is the most fuel-efficient car shown in this chart?

_____(1)   Volkswagen Rabbit diesel (5-speed)

_____(2)   Toyota Starlet (5-speed)

_____(3)   Volkswagen Rabbit diesel (4-speed)

_____(4)   Chevrolet Chevette

_____(5)   Mazda GLC (4-speed)

2. The three most fuel-efficient American cars are

_____(1)   Chevette, Escort and Lynx.

_____(2)   Dodge Colt, Plymouth Champ and Chevrolet Chevette.

_____(3)   Toyota, Honda and Mazda.

_____(4)   Ford, Chevrolet and Chrysler.

_____(5)   Datsun 210, Toyota Corolla Tercel and Ford Escort.

3.   How many miles to the gallon does the Dodge Colt (4-speed) get?

_____(1)   39

_____(2)   38

_____(3)   37

_____(4)   36

_____(5)   35

4.   Which three cars get 35 miles to a gallon of gas?

_____(1)   Datsun 210, Toyota Corolla Tercel and Honda Civic

_____(2)   Plymouth Champ, Dodge Colt and Volkswagen Rabbit

_____(3)   Chevrolet Chevette, Ford Escort and Lincoln-Mercury Lynx

_____(4)   Honda Civic, Mazda GLC (4-speed) and Mazda GLC (5-speed)

_____(5)   Volkswagen Rabbit (4-speed), Volkswagen Rabbit (5-speed) and Toyota Starlet (5-speed)

5.   How many cars on the chart get more than 35 miles per gallon?

_____(1)   10

_____(2)   13

_____(3)   6

_____(4)   8

_____(5)   7

ANSWERS AND EXPLANATIONS—PRACTICAL READING: ILLUSTRATIONS

Exercise 1

1. (2) heart, lungs and liver
2. (5) high blood pressure and high cholesterol
3. (2) the liver
4. (3) the lungs
5. (2) the spleen, stomach and gall bladder

Exercise 2

1. (3) how to use a fan during hot weather to cool your home.
2. (3) how cool air can move from a window through the rooms at night.
3. (4) Close all of them.
4. (4) facing an open bedroom window.
5. (3) blow the warm air out of your house.

Exercise 3

1. (2) how the fish are biting at different spots on Lake Kenny
2. (3) excellent fishing.
3. (1) Rainbow Bridge.
4. (5) Durango.
5. (4) at Hannah, Wyoming, below the dam.

Exercise 4

1. (2) a poll of Miller's High School students' favorite college basketball teams.
2. (3) DePaul
3. (4) wins so far this season
4. (1) 0
5. (5) 7

Exercise 5

1. (3) Trains from Clarksville to Monroe
2. (2) 12:45 P.M.
3. (3) Gate 8
4. (5) 6:15 A.M.
5. (2) Catch the 1:30 P.M. train at Gate 8.

Exercise 6

1. (5) Friday night TV listings.
2. (3) Charlie's Angels
3. (2) 6:00 P.M.
4. (3) Friday Night Movie—The Hunters (1974)
5. (3) Channel 11 at 6:30 P.M.
6. (1) News
7. (2) 2, 5, 7, 9 and 26
8. (3) Birth of the Blues (***)
9. (1) Midnight Special
10. (4) The Count of Monte Cristo, 9:00 P.M.

Exercise 7

1. (3) 30%
2. (4) 12%
3. (4) Food and household items and rent are the biggest slices and take up the same amount of income.
4. (2) savings; only 8% of the income goes to savings.
5. (5) $12,000

Exercise 8

1. (4) swimming
2. (3) four; tennis, camping, bicycling and swimming
3. (2) bowling, softball and skating
4. (1) 54,435,000
5. (4) bicycling

Exercise 9

1. (3) about 70 million
2. (1) 1930-1935, 1940-1945
3. (5) Overall, the number has increased.
4. (1) 60 million
5. (3) 80 million

Exercise 10

1. (3) 1940 and 1980.
2. (1) more people than Los Angeles.
3. (2) fewer people than Los Angeles.
4. (4) in 1960 and about 1973
5. (3) 1950-1960

ANSWERS AND EXPLANATIONS—REVIEW EXERCISES

Review Exercise 1

1. (2) government
2. (2) 17¢
3. (3) gifts
4. (4) Housing fees bring in more money than tuition.
5. (1) Tuition brings in more money than gifts.

Review Exercise 2

1. (2) teachers' salaries with master's degrees.
2. (2) $13,500
3. (5) $15,000
4. (4) four years
5. (3) $16,500

Review Exercise 3

1. (4) trains northbound from 10th Street to Madison.
2. (3) M-S 318
3. (1) eight stops including 10th Street and Madison.
4. (2) Notify the trainman.
5. (5) S-308

Review Exercise 4

1. (3) weather in the U.S. and Chicago temperatures.
2. (2) 25°
3. (1) Seattle

4. (4) 67° and 53°
5. (1) Chicago and New Orleans

Review Exercise 5

1. (1) the planets that orbit the sun.
2. (3) nine
3. (1) the sun and all bodies that circle it
4. (5) Pluto
5. (4) Saturn

Review Exercise 6

1. (3) Volkswagen Rabbit diesel (4-speed)
2. (1) Chevette, Escort and Lynx
3. (3) 37
4. (4) Honda Civic, Mazda GLC (4-speed) and Mazda GLC (5-speed)
5. (5) 7

POST-TEST

Look at the map on the following page. It shows you where to find Joe's Restaurant and Jim's Gameroom. Answer the questions about the map by checking the BEST choice.

1. What is the second street north of Joe's Restaurant?
   _____ (1)   Chestnut
   _____ (2)   Maple
   _____ (3)   Western
   _____ (4)   Oak
   _____ (5)   Spruce

2. Jim's Gameroom is directly south of which street?
   _____ (1)   Chestnut
   _____ (2)   Broadway
   _____ (3)   Division
   _____ (4)   King
   _____ (5)   Belmont

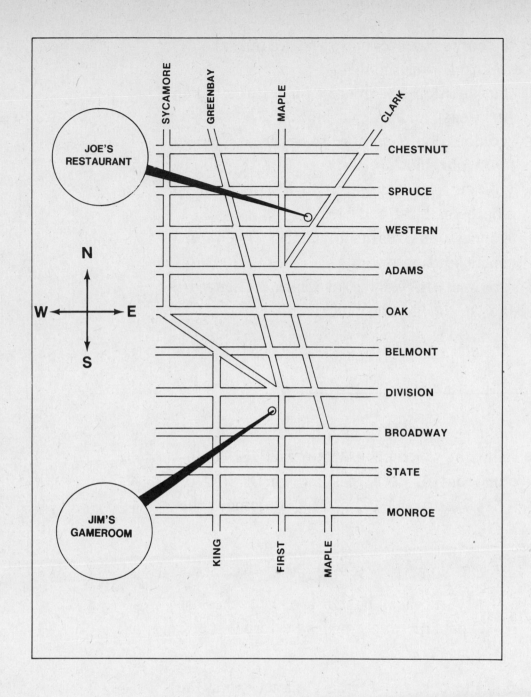

3. Only one street runs from the top of the map to the
    bottom. Which is it?

    _____ (1)   Greenbay
    _____ (2)   Sycamore
    _____ (3)   King
    _____ (4)   Clark
    _____ (5)   Maple

4. You are at the corner of Sycamore and Adams. To get
to Joe's Restaurant, you should

_____(1) go north on Sycamore to Chestnut. Then
turn east and go two blocks.

_____(2) go north on Sycamore to Spruce. Then go
west one block.

_____(3) go south on Sycamore to First. Then go
south on First one block.

_____(4) go east on Adams to Clark. Then turn
north and go one block.

_____(5) go west on Adams to Clark. Then turn
north and go one block.

Read each of the following sentences. Write "fact" or "opinion" in the blank in front of each to show which kind of
statement it is. Ask yourself, "Can this statement be
proved?"

_____ 5. My mother baked three batches of
chocolate chip cookies yesterday.

_____ 6. Pluto is the furthest planet from the
sun.

_____ 7. January is the most unpleasant month
of the year.

_____ 8. Redheads should wear green.

_____ 9. China has more people than any other
country on Earth.

_____10. Spinach is the only vegetable that tastes bad.

_____11. Having no money isn't bad if you have a loving family.

_____12. A mother shouldn't work until her children are in school.

_____13. Most American women have jobs.

_____14. Cigarette smoking is bad for your health.

_____

Read the graph and check the correct answers in the following.

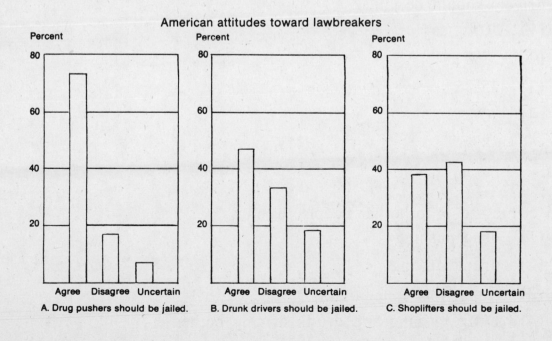

American attitudes toward lawbreakers

A. Drug pushers should be jailed.

B. Drunk drivers should be jailed.

C. Shoplifters should be jailed.

15. About what percentage of Americans think drug pushers should be put in jail?

_____(1)   72%

_____(2)   80%

_____(3)   20%

_____(4)   18%

_____(5)   60%

16. About what percentage of Americans think shoplifters should not be put in jail?

_____(1)   40%

_____(2)   42%

_____(3)   50%

_____(4)   38%

_____(5)   18%

17. About what percentage of people are not sure whether drunk drivers should be jailed?

_____(1)   30%

_____(2)   28%

_____(3)   25%

_____(4)   20%

_____(5)   18%

18. Which crime seems to bother people the most?

_____(1)   drug pushing

_____(2)   drunk driving

_____(3)   shoplifting

_____(4)   Drug pushing and drunk driving bother people the same amount.

_____(5)   You can't tell from the graph.

19. Which crime seems to bother people the least?

_____(1)   drug pushing

_____(2)   drunk driving

_____(3)   shoplifting

_____(4)   Drug pushing and drunk driving bother people least.

_____(5)   You can't tell from the graph.

Installing the Storm-Air Screen

The Storm-Air screen you've just bought is a recent development of Industrial Laboratories, Inc. It will let you enjoy open windows on stormy or rainy nights. The Storm-Air lets the cool air enter your room. But it stops the rain from ruining your sills, floors, or furniture.

The Storm-Air comes in two types, Model A and Model B. Model A is for older homes with pull-up windows. Model B is for the newer roll-out or sliding windows.

The Storm-Air screen is made of dozens of small aluminum bands. These bands are shaped like eaves on a roof. (See Figure A.) They allow the air to come in but catch the water.

Your Storm-Air comes in three pieces. These are wide enough for all windows. Each piece is six inches high.

If you want your window open only six inches, pull it up. Then put in one piece of the Storm-Air screen. (See Figure B.)

THE STORM-AIR SCREEN: MODEL A

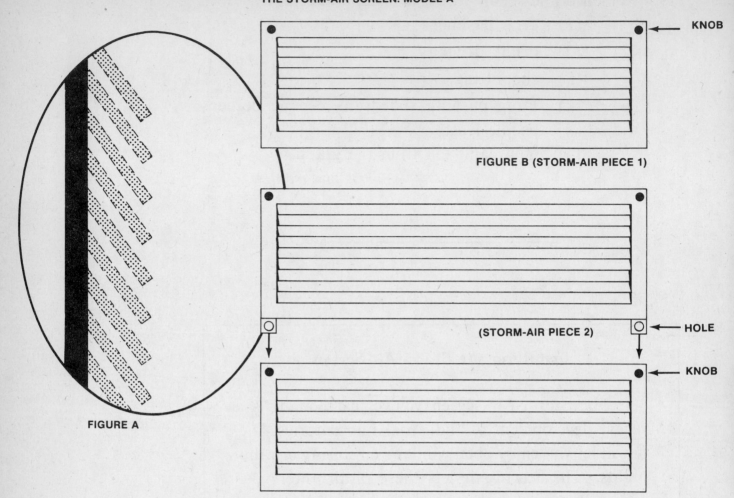

FIGURE A

KNOB

FIGURE B (STORM-AIR PIECE 1)

(STORM-AIR PIECE 2)

HOLE

KNOB

FIGURE C (STORM-AIR PIECE 2)

If you want a bigger opening, attach a second piece of the screen to the first one. The knobs at the bottom of the screen will snap into the holes at the top of the first piece.

This will give you an opening of 12 inches. A third piece makes an 18-inch opening. (See Figure C.)

Your Storm-Air is made of lightweight aluminum. It will not rust. After each use, wipe the Storm-Air with a soft cloth. This will help you get years of trouble-free use.

Be sure also to store the Storm-Air on its edges. Never place it flat. Keep Storm-Air screens away from things that could dent them.

Put a check in front of the best ending for each sentence.

20. The Storm-Air screen was developed to

_____(1) keep out mosquitoes and flies.

_____(2) keep out cold, icy winds.

_____(3) keep out rain on a stormy night.

_____(4) keep out dust on windy days.

_____(5) all of the above

21. The Storm-Air screen comes in

_____(1) Models A and B.

_____(2) Models A, B and C.

_____(3) pull-ups, roll-outs and sliding models.

_____(4) Models B and C.

_____(5) four different pieces—A, B, C and D.

22. The Model described here is

_____(1) Model C.

_____(2) Model B.

_____(3) Model D.

_____(4) Model A.

_____(5) all of the above

23. The Storm-Air screen itself is made of

_____(1) a copper bug screening.

_____(2) a fine mesh to hold back water.

_____(3) dozens of aluminum bands.

_____(4) dozens of stainless-steel bands.

_____(5) none of the above

24. The Storm-Air screen is built like

_____(1) the gutter on a roof.

_____(2) the eaves of a roof.

_____(3)   rainspouts on a roof.

_____(4)   the shingles on a roof.

_____(5)   none of the above

25.   The smallest opening you can make with a Storm-Air
       screen is
       _____(1)   10 inches.
       _____(2)   18 inches.
       _____(3)   12 inches.
       _____(4)   6 inches.
       _____(5)   none of the above

26.   The largest opening possible with a Storm-Air screen is
       _____(1)   10 inches.
       _____(2)   18 inches.
       _____(3)   12 inches.
       _____(4)   6 inches.
       _____(5)   none of the above

27.   To put the pieces of the Storm-Air screen together, you
       must
       _____(1)   screw the bottom of one to the top of the
                     other.
       _____(2)   insert pins into the bottom of one and the
                     top of the other.
       _____(3)   snap the bottom of one onto the bottom of
                     the other.
       _____(4)   use copper keys on the bottom of one and
                     the top of the other.
       _____(5)   none of the above

28.   Because the Storm-Air is made of aluminum, it won't
       _____(1)   rust.
       _____(2)   break.
       _____(3)   dent.

_____(4) lose color.

_____(5) all of the above

29. When not in use, the Storm-Air should be

_____(1) stored flat.

_____(2) kept away from other aluminum objects.

_____(3) stored in a dry place.

_____(4) stored on its edges.

_____(5) none of the above

Read this passage. Watch for the speaker's bias. Then answer the questions that follow.

Yes, my wife and kids and I like to "rough it" when we go on vacation. Some people like to take it easy. But we really prefer getting out there and living like the pioneers.

Oh sure, we recently bought a new trailer. There's a bed for each of us; hot and cold running water; a refrigerator, but no freezer; and a gas stove. It has its own little generator for lights. We take a couple of small television sets when we go, just in case we want to watch different programs, you know.

The bathroom? Oh no! That's part of "roughing it." We go to state parks where there are public bathrooms and showers. They're very nice—all tile and brick. The parks people keep them very clean, too.

No, nobody ever bothers us. Except sometimes we have to tell some people to get away from the showers. You know, those people who live like animals. They just put packs on their backs and go off and sleep under trees and cook on wood fires! They come around once in a while. I can't imagine how people can stoop so low.

30. The speaker and his family like to "rough it," he says. What does he think "roughing it" means? What things must he have around him?

     _____(1)   a bed for each person

     _____(2)   hot and cold water

     _____(3)   a couple of small television sets

     _____(4)   a gas stove

     _____(5)   all of the above

31. Which of these things can the speaker do without while "roughing it"?

     _____(1)   a stove

     _____(2)   a freezer

     _____(3)   a bathroom

     _____(4)   a small television set

     _____(5)   all of the above

32. Which one of these is the speaker's opinion of people who put packs on their backs?

     _____(1)   They really know how to camp.

     _____(2)   They are nice people who have a different way of camping.

     _____(3)   He looks down on them.

     _____(4)   He doesn't care how they camp.

     _____(5)   none of the above

33. Which one of these points could be a fact?

     _____(1)   I can't imagine how people can stoop so low.

     _____(2)   Those people live like animals.

     _____(3)   Most people like to take it easy.

     _____(4)   We recently bought a new trailer.

     _____(5)   none of the above

ANSWERS AND EXPLANATIONS—POST-TEST

1. (1) Chestnut
2. (3) Division
3. (5) Maple
4. (4) Go east on Adams to Clark. Then turn north and go one block.

5. Fact. This statement can be checked and proved.
6. Fact. This statement can be checked and proved.
7. Opinion. This is a statement of opinion. We could not prove it to be true. People would have different opinions.
8. Opinion. There could be different feelings about this statement. It cannot be proved.
9. Fact. This statement could be proved.
10. Opinion. Some people might like the taste of spinach.
11. Opinion. This is a matter of the writer's or speaker's opinion.
12. Opinion. Someone could make the opposite statement and feel that it was right.
13. Fact. We could look up the numbers and check this statement.
14. Fact. According to the U.S. Surgeon General this is a fact.

15. (1) 72%
16. (2) 42%
17. (5) 18%
18. (1) drug pushing
19. (3) shoplifting

20. (3) The instructions say that the screen was made to keep out rain.

21. (1) There are two types, Model A and Model B. Each model comes in 3 pieces.

22. (4) The diagram tells us that this is Model A which is for older homes with pull-up windows.

23. (3) The Storm-Air screen is made of dozens of small aluminum bands.

24. (2) The Storm-Air screen is built like the eaves of a roof. Also see Figure A.

25. (4) Each Storm-Air screen piece is 6 inches high. If only one piece is used, there would be an opening of 6 inches.

26. (2) If all three pieces are used, there would be an opening of 18 inches.

27. (3) The knobs at the bottom of one piece snap into the holes at the top of another piece.

28. (1) We are told that the screens are made of aluminum and that they will not rust.

29. (4) The last paragraph of the instructions says the screen should be stored on its edges.

30. (5) All of the above. The speaker mentioned (1), (2), (3) and (4) as part of "roughing it."

31. (2) a freezer. The refrigerator has no freezer. (1) and (4) are things the family takes with them. As for (3), they only go to campgrounds that have public bathrooms.

32. (3) He looks down on them. He says they live like animals.

33. (4) We recently bought a new trailer. This point can easily be proved. The others are points of opinion.

POST-TEST SKILL MASTERY CHART

Directions: Fill in the Skill Mastery Chart after you have checked your work on the Post-Test. Each skill on the test is listed with the test questions using that skill. Circle each question you answered correctly. Then count your total number of circled answers and write this in the box under Number Correct. Next, find the Skill Mastery Level that fits your number correct. Place a check ($\checkmark$) in the box at the right level. Do this for each skill listed. Then find your total number of correct answers and total number of checks at each Skill Mastery Level. Compare your results on the Post-Test with what you did on the Pre-Test Skill Mastery Chart. Both charts will show you what your next step should be in building your reading skills.

SKILL	TOTAL SCORE	NUMBER CORRECT	SKILL MASTERY LEVELS			STUDY PAGES
			SKILL MASTERY	PRACTICE & REVIEW NEEDED	FULL LEARNING NEEDED	
			(Check one box in each row)			
1 Critical Reading 5, 6, 7, 8, 9 10, 11, 12, 13, 14	14		14-9	8-5	4-0	13-52
2 Following Directions 20, 21, 22, 23, 24 25, 26, 27, 28, 29	10		10-8	7-4	3-0	53-94
3 Charts/Graphs/Diagrams 1, 2, 3, 4 15, 16, 17, 18, 19	9		9-7	6-4	3-0	95-137
TOTAL	33					